THE FRUIT OF THE SPIRIT
A Gospel Perspective

setting
CAPTIVES free

THE FRUIT OF
THE SPIRIT

— A Gospel Perspective —

BILL MILLER

SETTING CAPTIVES FREE
PUBLISHING

Setting Captives Free Publishing
Jackson, WY

ISBN: 978-1-7337609-9-7
LCCN: 2021921556

Table of Contents

Acknowledgments

*O*ver the past few years, the Lord has helped me see the centrality of the Gospel, Jesus' death, burial, and resurrection, in all of Scripture. In addition, the Board members at Setting Captives Free (Mike Cleveland, Petrus Zijlstra, Rob Robertson, and Erick Hurt) have faithfully modeled what it means to be Cross-focused. As a result, I have become more convinced that understanding the Scriptures correctly is through the lens of the Gospel. So, I ask myself: "How does this Scripture point me to Jesus and the Cross?"

My elder at church, Jerold Barnett, asked if I would teach the adult Sunday School. He specifically requested that I teach on the Fruit of the Spirit from Galatians 5:22-23. He cheered me on each week. I accepted the honor to teach God's word to the people. I came with one focus, "Jesus Christ and Him crucified."

My pastor, Clarence Veld, has been a great encouragement, and his faithful preaching of the Word each Sunday morning and evening always brought out the centrality of the Gospel in the text. In addition, he was modeling for me the importance of seeing Jesus and the Cross in every sermon. Sometimes, we would talk about my lesson the week before, which helped clarify the pointing to Jesus.

My wife, Diane, has always been a great support and allowed me the study time to prepare and present these lessons to the glory of God.

My greatest blessing in preparing these lessons has been the Lord. At the beginning of each week, I would pray, "Help me see Jesus in that part of the Fruit." Then, each week the Holy Spirit would lead me to a particular cross-reference verse that would say, "Look, there is Jesus!" Then my focus was on Jesus with that characteristic of the Fruit of the Spirit for that week's study being displayed from the Cross.

Overview

*G*reetings friend,

My name is Bill Miller; I will be walking with you through the 13 lessons in this study, and I'm praying that the Holy Spirit will show you how being crucified with Jesus Christ will bring about the fruit of the Spirit in your life.

These lessons came out of my time of study for teaching a Bible study at my church. I have been a Christian for over 50 years and through the years I have read many times the fruit of the Spirit listed in Galatians 5.

> *"But the fruit of the Spirit is love, joy, peace, longsuffering, kindness, goodness, faithfulness, (23) gentleness, self-control. Against such there is no law." (Galatians 5:22-23 NKJV)*

But I never studied these verses in the context of the Gospel, Jesus' death, burial, and resurrection. Come with me as we study the fruit of the Spirit here at the foot of the Cross. As you look up and consider Jesus, you will begin to see Jesus living and dying with these qualities in His life. My prayer is that you will also be transformed into that same image of our Lord.

> *"But we all, with unveiled face, beholding as in a mirror the glory of the Lord, are being transformed into the same image from glory to glory, just as by the Spirit of the Lord." (2 Corinthians 3:18 NKJV)*

My hope is that you will be in God's word daily and finish this study with a new understanding of the power of the Gospel, working itself out in the Fruit of the Spirit. It is best to take your time so that you can assimilate the truths and apply them to your life. Be thoughtful about your answers. Try not to give one word or one-sentence answers.

As we begin, we will cover these four areas in the first lesson:

- Who has the Holy Spirit?
- How do we receive the Holy Spirit?
- Compare and contrast works of the flesh and the fruit of the Spirit.
- What is our only hope?

Who Has the Holy Spirit?
Before we start talking about the Fruit of the Spirit, we need to ask, "Who has the Holy Spirit?" Let's look at several verses in the Bible to help us answer that question.

> "On the last day, that great day of the feast, Jesus stood and cried out, saying, "If anyone thirsts, let him come to Me and drink. He who believes in Me, as the Scripture has said, out of his heart will flow rivers of living water." [Then John adds this commentary] But this He spoke concerning the Spirit, whom those believing in Him would receive; for the Holy Spirit was not yet given, because Jesus was not yet glorified." John 7:37-39 (NKJV)

Those who believe in Him would receive the Holy Spirit. We need to start with the Gospel to understand who it is that we are believing.

LET'S DEFINE THE GOSPEL: 1 CORINTHIANS 15:1-4

> "Moreover, brethren, I declare to you the gospel which I preached to you, which also you received and in which you stand, by which also you are saved, if you hold fast that word which I preached to you—unless you believed in vain. For I delivered to you first of all that which I also received: that Christ died for our sins according to the Scriptures, and that He was buried, and that He rose again the third day according to the Scriptures," 1 Corinthians 15:1-4 (NKJV)

Question 1: How does Paul define the Gospel?

☐ God loves you and has a wonderful plan for your life.

☐ Jesus' death, burial, and resurrection.

☐ The whole Bible is the Gospel.

Yes, the Gospel is defined as the death of Jesus Christ for our sins, His burial, and His resurrection from the dead on the third day. Not only is the Gospel necessary to believe for our salvation, but it is also to be believed for our sanctification.

Paul wrote to the Christians in Rome and had planned to come and visit them. He wanted to be encouraged together with them because of the mutual faith. *(Romans 1:12-14)* Then Paul says some wonderful things to the Christians at Rome concerning the Gospel:

> *"So, as much as is in me, I am ready to preach the gospel to you who are in Rome also. (16) For I am not ashamed of the gospel of Christ, for it is the power of God to salvation for everyone who believes, for the Jew first and for the Greek. (17) For in it, the righteousness of God is revealed from faith to faith; as it is written, "The just shall live by faith." (Romans 1:15-17 NKJV)*

Question 2: What characteristics do we see about the Gospel?

_____

_____

_____

_____

_____

Yes, these are the characteristics of the Gospel.

It is to be preached to believers. <u>Do not miss this point, the Gospel is not merely for the unbeliever – it is for the Christian.</u> It is through the message of the Gospel and its application we grow in the grace and knowledge of our Lord Jesus.

It is the power of God to salvation to everyone who believes. What do they believe? Jesus' death, burial, and resurrection for themselves personally.

Then in verse 17, Paul goes on to say that the Gospel is for ongoing sanctification, *"For in it (the Gospel)* **the righteousness of God is revealed from faith to faith***."* As we see Jesus dying on the Cross for our sins, we see Him being buried in that tomb; we see Him rising from the dead, we see God's righteousness is being revealed. From faith to faith, we grow in the grace and knowledge of our Lord and Savior, Jesus Christ. *(2 Peter 3:18)*

As we consider the Gospel, the message of the Cross is foolishness to those who are perishing. But to us who are being saved, it is the power of God. Notice the centrality of the Gospel in Paul's thinking in 1 Corinthians 1:18-25.

> *"For the message of the cross is foolishness to those who are perishing, but to us who are being saved, it is the power of God. (19) For it is written: "I will destroy the wisdom of the wise, And bring to nothing the understanding of the prudent." (20) Where is the wise? Where is the scribe? Where is the disputer of this age? Has not God made foolish the wisdom of this world? (21) For since, in the wisdom of God, the world through wisdom did not know God, it pleased God through the foolishness of the message preached to save those who believe. (22) For Jews request a sign, and Greeks seek after wisdom; (23) but we preach Christ crucified, to the Jews a stumbling block and to the Greeks foolishness, (24) but to those who are called, both Jews and Greeks, Christ the power of God and the wisdom of God. (25) Because the foolishness of God is wiser than men, and the weakness of God is stronger than men." (1 Corinthians 1:18-25 NKJV)*

Question 3: How is the message of the Cross contrasted with the wisdom of the world?

_____

_____

_____

_____

_____

The Cross – offers wisdom and the power of God to save those who believe.
    The world – offers foolishness, unable to know God.
    When Paul came to the Christians at Corinth, he had only one message:

> *"And I, brethren, when I came to you, did not come with excellence of speech or of wisdom declaring to you the testimony of God. (2) For I determined not to know anything among you except Jesus Christ and Him crucified." (1 Corinthians 2:1-2 NKJV)*

Paul only had this one message and applied that message of the Gospel (Jesus' death, burial, and resurrection) to all of life. That message of "Jesus Christ and Him crucified" was not in words of human wisdom, but in demonstration of the Spirit and of power. (1 Corinthians 2:4) Why? So, your faith should not be in the wisdom of men but the power of God. (1 Corinthians 2:5).

**The power of God to live the Christian life is found in the Gospel.**

Through this message of the Gospel, we also receive the Holy Spirit when we believe.

How do we receive the Holy Spirit?
Now let's go back to what Jesus said about the Holy Spirit:

"On the last day, that great day of the feast, Jesus stood and cried out, saying, "If anyone thirsts, let him come to Me and drink. He who believes in Me, as the Scripture has said, out of his heart will flow rivers of living water." But this He spoke concerning the Spirit, whom those believing in Him would receive; for the Holy Spirit was not yet given, because Jesus was not yet glorified." John 7:37-39 (NKJV)

Question 4: According to John 7:37-39, what happens to the person who comes and believes in Jesus?
- ☐ Out of their heart will flow rivers of living water. This Jesus spoke concerning the Spirit.
- ☐ They will get a feeling of happiness.
- ☐ They will join the church and read the Bible.

Yes, something happens to our heart; it will flow rivers of living water. And John adds his commentary as to what that means: the believer would receive the Holy Spirit. The Holy Spirit will be a flow of living water within the believer.

Paul tells us at what point we receive the Holy Spirit:

Read Ephesians 1:1-12 for context and list all the benefits of believing the Gospel, the word of truth.

"(1) Paul, an apostle of Jesus Christ by the will of God, To the saints who are in Ephesus, and faithful in Christ Jesus: (2) Grace to you and peace from God our Father and the Lord Jesus Christ.

(3) Blessed be the God and Father of our Lord Jesus Christ, who has blessed us with every spiritual blessing in the heavenly places in Christ, (4) just as He chose us in Him before the foundation of the world, that we should be holy and without blame before Him in love, (5) having predestined us to adoption as sons by Jesus Christ to Himself, according to the good pleasure of His will, (6) to the praise of the glory of His grace, by which He made us accepted in the Beloved.

(7) In Him we have redemption through His blood, the forgiveness of sins, according to the riches of His grace (8) which He made to abound toward us in all wisdom and prudence, (9) having made known to us the mystery of His will, according to His good pleasure which He purposed in Himself, (10) that in the dispensation of the fullness of the times He might gather together in one all things in Christ, both which are in heaven and which are on earth--in Him. (11) In Him also we have obtained an inheritance, being predestined according to the purpose of Him who works all things according to the counsel of His will, (12) that we who first trusted in Christ should be to the praise of His glory." (Ephesians 1:1-12 NKJV)

And how do we receive all these benefits? Keep reading:

"(13) In Him you also trusted, after you heard the word of truth, the gospel of your salvation; in whom also, having believed, you were sealed with the Holy Spirit of promise, (14) who is the guarantee of our inheritance until the redemption of the purchased possession, to the praise of His glory." (Ephesians 1:13-14 NKJV)

Question 5: According to Paul in Ephesians 1:1-14, list everything that happens when someone believes the word of truth, the Gospel?

_____

_____

_____

_____

_____

Here is the list of benefits that I found:

- Blessed with every spiritual blessing in the heavenly places
- Be holy and without blame before Him in love
- Adopted by Jesus Christ to Himself
- Made accepted in the Beloved
- Redemption through His blood
- Forgiveness of sins
- Know the mystery of His will (the Gospel)
- Obtained an inheritance
- Salvation
- Sealed with the Holy Spirit who is the guarantee of our inheritance

Yes, those trusting in Jesus and believe the Gospel (Jesus' death, burial, and resurrection) will be saved and sealed with the Holy Spirit. The Holy Spirit is God's guarantee of our inheritance and salvation.

We are being blessed with the promise of Abraham because through faith in Christ Jesus, we received the promise of the Spirit.

> *"that the blessing of Abraham might come upon the Gentiles in Christ Jesus, that we might receive the promise of the Spirit through faith." (Galatians 3:14 NKJV)*

Compare the works of the Flesh vs. the Fruit of the Spirit.
Galatians 5:16-26 will help us as we focus on the fruit of the Spirit and contrast this fruit with the works of the flesh.

We are in a real battle between our flesh and the Spirit:

> *"I say then: Walk in the Spirit, and you shall not fulfill the lust of the flesh. (17) For the flesh lusts against the Spirit, and the Spirit against the flesh; and these are contrary to one another, so that you do not do the things that you wish. (18) But if you are led by the Spirit, you are not under the law." (Galatians 5:16-18 NKJV)*

We see Paul describing this battle in Romans 7:7-25. For the Christian, there is a real struggle with sin. Our flesh wants to do one thing, and the Holy Spirit leads us to do something else.

Question 6: What contrast do we see between walking in the Spirit and fulfilling the lust of the flesh in Galatians 5:16-18?

_____

_____

_____

_____

_____

Yes, there is a battle going on with the Christian. However, when we are walking in the Spirit and being led by the Spirit, we are not fulfilling the lust of the flesh, and we are not under the law. As we return to the Cross, we look up and see that our old man has been crucified with Christ, and by the power of the Gospel, we live from faith to faith.

Let's take a quick look at the works of the flesh that Paul lists here in Galatians 5:19-21.

> *"Now the works of the flesh are evident, which are: adultery, fornication, uncleanness, lewdness, (20) idolatry, sorcery, hatred, contentions, jealousies, outbursts of wrath, selfish ambitions, dissensions, heresies, (21) envy, murders, drunkenness, revelries, and the like; of which I tell you beforehand, just as I also told you in time past, that those who practice such things will not inherit the kingdom of God." (Galatians 5:19-21 NKJV)*

> *"Now the practices of the sinful nature are clearly evident: they are sexual immorality, impurity, sensuality (total irresponsibility, lack of self-control), idolatry, sorcery, hostility, strife, jealousy, fits of anger, disputes, dissensions, factions [that promote heresies], envy, drunkenness, riotous behavior, and other things like these. I warn you beforehand, just as I did previously, that those who practice*

such things will not inherit the kingdom of God." Galatians 5:19-21 (AMP)

- **Adultery** – unfaithful to the marriage vows
- **Fornication** – any sexual sins (pornography, self-gratification, homosexuality, any sexual intercourse – physical or mental)
- **Uncleanness** – impurity of lustful, luxurious living, defiled by worldly thinking
- **Lewdness** – unbridled lust, filthy language, disgraceful, uncontrolled tongue
- **Idolatry** – worship false gods, the sin of the mind (putting X over God – X: job, family, recreation, sports, TV, games, eating, etc.)
- **Sorcery** – pharmakeía – use of drugs, witchcraft, occult, use the devil for gain
- **Hatred** – enmity, hostility, Opposite of agapé love
- **Contentions** – strife, quarreling, debating,
- **Jealousies** – zeal, defending anything of self, rivalry with others,
- **Outbursts of Wrath** – passion, anger, inflamed indignation,
- **Selfish Ambitions** – the self-seeking pursuit of politics, "party spirit," I'm the best.
- **Dissensions** – causing divisions, standing apart,
- **Heresies** – self-willed opinion over truth
- **Envy** – spiteful jealousy, the displeasure of others' prosperity, want to deprive others of what they have.
- **Murders** – slaughter or killing a human person
- **Drunkenness** – méthē: intoxication, in bondage to alcohol,
- **Revelries** - carousal (letting loose), partying (food and drink) all night, rioting, riotous living
- **And the Like** – if Paul missed anything: resembling anything from the above list.

Those who habitually practice these things will not inherit the kingdom of God. It is not saying that a Christian who struggles is disqualified for heaven, but the one who has no regard for God and would rather stay in their sin – is not a Christian.

Question 7: Have you seen any of the works of the flesh in your own life? Are you aware of any of these in your life right now, and you cannot break free?

_____

_____

_____

_____

_____

_____

What is our only hope?

Yes, as long as we are in these sinful bodies, we will have this conflict going on within our lives. But the Good News is found in Galatians 5:24-25:

> *"And those who are Christ's have crucified the flesh with its passions and desires. (25) If we live in the Spirit, let us also walk in the Spirit." (Galatians 5:24-25 NKJV)*

There is real hope to overcome and put to death the "old man." We come to the Cross and find ourselves crucified with Christ. We will find our freedom in the Gospel, not only for our salvation but also for our sanctification.

Paul shows us from these verses and in Galatians 2:20-21 the key to exhibiting the fruit of the Spirit:

> *"I have been crucified with Christ; it is no longer I who live, but Christ lives in me; and the life which I now live in the flesh I live by faith in the Son of God, who loved me and gave Himself for me. (21) "I do not set aside the grace of God; for if righteousness comes through the law, then Christ died in vain." (Galatians 2:20-21 NKJV)*

Question 8: Have you come to the place where you have believed the Gospel? Have you believed and have put your faith in the death, burial, and resurrection of Jesus Christ? Do you desire to walk in the Spirit? Please explain.

We will find that the fruit of the Spirit are those qualities that we see in Jesus Himself. So next lesson, we will begin looking at these qualities of the fruit that are found in Christ and manifesting in our lives.

> *"But the fruit of the Spirit is love, joy, peace, longsuffering, kindness, goodness, faithfulness, (23) gentleness, self-control. Against such there is no law." (Galatians 5:22-23 NKJV)*

Love

Welcome back. I am looking forward to studying this characteristic of the Fruit of the Spirit: Love.

The fruit of the Spirit in Galatians 5:22-23 is in the context of the battle going on within the Christian.

> *"I say then: Walk in the Spirit, and you shall not fulfill the lust of the flesh. (17) For the flesh lusts against the Spirit, and the Spirit against the flesh; and these are contrary to one another so that you do not do the things that you wish. (18) But if you are led by the Spirit, you are not under the law. ...*

Paul gives a list of the works of the flesh then says, BUT....

> *(22) But the fruit of the Spirit is love, joy, peace, longsuffering, kindness, goodness, faithfulness, (23) gentleness, self-control. Against such, there is no law." (Galatians 5:16-18, 22-23 NKJV)*

And Paul brings the discussion back to the Gospel, back to the Cross:

> *"And those who are Christ's have crucified the flesh with its passions and desires. (25) If we live in the Spirit, let us also walk in the Spirit. (26) Let us not become conceited, provoking one another, envying one another." (Galatians 5:24-26 NKJV)*

Introduction: Walking in the Spirit in love
We are going to look at three points:

- We are going to define love in different relationships.
- Look at an example of God's love from the Old Testament that reflects the Gospel.
- Showing how the Cross demonstrates love.

Let's look at the first quality of the Fruit of the Spirit: Love

Let's define this word Love
ἀγάπη **agape:** affection, goodwill, love, benevolence, brotherly love

I found "Agape and agapao is used in the NT in at least five different ways:

1. To describe the attitude and love of God the Father toward God the Son, Jesus.

> *"And suddenly a voice came from heaven, saying, "This is My beloved Son, in whom I am well pleased." (Matthew 3:17 NKJV)*

At Jesus' baptism, The Father speaks from heaven – this is my beloved.

> *"While he was still speaking, behold, a bright cloud overshadowed them; and suddenly a voice came out of the cloud, saying, "This is My beloved Son, in whom I am well pleased. Hear Him!" (Matthew 17:5 NKJV)*

There on the Mount Transfiguration, The Father speaks from heaven – How much do these reflect the Old Testament prophecy?

> *"Behold! My Servant whom I uphold, My Elect One in whom My soul delights! I have put My Spirit upon Him; He will bring forth justice to the Gentiles." (Isaiah 42:1 NKJV)*

How is this justice brought forth? Jesus went to the Cross and laid down His life. The Father's love for a Son who delights His soul because He did that which was right.

Jesus reminded the disciples how He loved them by comparison:

"As the Father loved Me, I also have loved you; abide in My love."
(John 15:9 NKJV)

Even in Jesus' High Priestly pray in John 17, He reflects on the Father's love:

"I in them, and You in Me; that they may be made perfect in one, and that the world may know that You have sent Me, and have loved them as You have loved Me. ... (26) "And I have declared to them Your name, and will declare it, that the love with which You loved Me may be in them, and I in them." (John 17:23, 26 NKJV)

Question 1: How do you see God the Father, loving Jesus in the above verses?

_____

_____

_____

_____

_____

2. God's general love toward humanity.

"You have heard that it was said, 'You shall love your neighbor and hate your enemy.' (44) "But I say to you, love your enemies, bless those who curse you, do good to those who hate you, and pray for those who spitefully use you and persecute you, (45) "that you may be sons of your Father in heaven; for He makes His sun rise on the evil and on the good, and sends rain on the just and on the unjust. (46) "For if you love those who love you, what reward have you? Do not even the tax collectors do the same? (47) "And if you greet your brethren only, what do you

do more than others? Do not even the tax collectors do so? (48)
"Therefore, you shall be perfect, just as your Father in heaven is
perfect." (Matthew 5:43-48 NKJV)

"For God so loved the world that He gave His only begotten
Son, that whoever believes in Him should not perish but have
everlasting life." (John 3:16 NKJV)

God's love for humanity does not negate God's justice and holiness. If you
refuse to believe what Jesus did at the Cross and His resurrection – there is
no other way.

"He who believes in the Son has everlasting life; and he who does
not believe the Son shall not see life, but the wrath of God abides
on him." (John 3:36 NKJV)

Question 2: How do you see God loving humanity in general in the above verses?
- ☐ God loves everyone; therefore, everyone will go to heaven.
- ☐ Only a person who keeps the commandments will go to heaven.
- ☐ Even though God loves humanity, only those who believe in the
  Son will go to heaven.

3. God's particular love toward those who believe in the Lord Jesus Christ.

"He who has My commandments and keeps them, it is he who loves
Me. And he who loves Me will be loved by My Father, and I will
love him and manifest Myself to him." (22) Judas (not Iscariot)
said to Him, "Lord, how is it that You will manifest Yourself to
us, and not to the world?" (23) Jesus answered and said to him,
"If anyone loves Me, he will keep My word; and My Father will
love him, and We will come to him and make Our home with
him." (John 14:21-23 NKJV)

How can we keep Jesus' commandments?

"For when we were still without strength, in due time, Christ died for the ungodly. (7) For scarcely for a righteous man will one die; yet perhaps for a good man, someone would even dare to die. (8) But God demonstrates His own love toward us, in that while we were still sinners, Christ died for us." (Romans 5:6-8 NKJV)

This is the Gospel for us - Jesus kept the commandments for us and died in our place.

"And walk in love, as Christ also has loved us and given Himself for us, an offering and a sacrifice to God for a sweet-smelling aroma." (Ephesians 5:2 NKJV)

"This is how we have discovered love's reality: Jesus sacrificed his life for us. Because of this great love, we should be willing to lay down our lives for one another." 1 John 3:16 (TPT)

Jesus became our sacrifice and died for our sins.

"In this, the love of God was manifested toward us, that God has sent His only begotten Son into the world, that we might live through Him. (10) In this is love, not that we loved God, but that He loved us and sent His Son to be the propitiation for our sins." (1 John 4:9-10 NKJV)

Question 3: How do you see God loving the believer in the above verses?

_____

_____

_____

_____

_____

4. This love of God conveys His will to His children concerning their attitude toward other Christians and toward all men.

Love should be a part of the fruit of the Spirit in the Christian's life. Galatians 5:22.

> *"A new commandment I give to you, that you love one another; as I have loved you, that you also love one another. (35) "By this, all will know that you are My disciples, if you have love for one another." (John 13:34-35 NKJV)*

> *"And may the Lord make you increase and abound in love to one another and to all, just as we do to you" (1 Thessalonians 3:12 NKJV)*

> *"This is My commandment, that you love one another as I have loved you. (13) "Greater love has no one than this, than to lay down one's life for his friends." (John 15:12-13 NKJV)*

We measure our love by looking at the Cross – do I love like that?

> *"Love suffers long and is kind; love does not envy; love does not parade itself, is not puffed up; (5) does not behave rudely, does not seek its own, is not provoked, thinks no evil; (6) does not rejoice in iniquity, but rejoices in the truth; (7) bears all things, believes all things, hopes all things, endures all things. Love never fails" (1 Corinthians 13:4-8 NKJV)*

Question 4: How do we see God's love being expressed through the believer in the above verses?

_____

_____

_____

_____

_____

5. Christian-love has God for its primary object and expresses itself first in implicit obedience to His commandments,

> *"If you love Me, keep My commandments. ... (21) "He who has My commandments and keeps them, it is he who loves Me. And he who loves Me will be loved by My Father, and I will love him and manifest Myself to him."... (23) Jesus answered and said to him, "If anyone loves Me, he will keep My word; and My Father will love him, and We will come to him and make Our home with him. (John 14:15,21,23 NKJV)*

> *"If you keep My commandments, you will abide in My love, just as I have kept My Father's commandments and abide in His love. (John 15:10 NKJV)*

Only Jesus kept the Father's commandment to fulfill the whole law and go to the Cross to die for unworthy sinners. By faith, we love and obey – Because Jesus did. So, we walk, not perfectly – but we walk with Him.

> *"He who says, "I know Him," and does not keep His commandments, is a liar, and the truth is not in him. (5) But whoever keeps His word, truly the love of God is perfected in him. By this we know that we are in Him. (6) He who says he abides in Him ought*

himself also to walk just as He walked." (1 John 2:4-6 NKJV)

Earlier, John said:

> *"But if we walk in the light as He is in the light, we have fellowship with one another, and the blood of Jesus Christ His Son cleanses us from all sin." (1 John 1:7 NKJV)*

It is the blood that cleanses as we walk daily there at the foot of the Cross. And our walk is also with fellow believers.

> *"Whoever believes that Jesus is the Christ is born of God, and everyone who loves Him who begot also loves him who is begotten of Him. (2) By this we know that we love the children of God, when we love God and keep His commandments. (3) For this is the love of God, that we keep His commandments. And His commandments are not burdensome." (1 John 5:1-3 NKJV)*

Question 5: How do we see the believer loving God in the above verses?

_____

_____

_____

_____

_____

Conclusion and summary of Love
Self-will that is, self-pleasing, is the negation of love to God.

Whether exercised toward fellow Christians or people generally, Christian love is not an impulse from the feelings. It does not always run with the natural inclinations, nor does it spend itself only upon those for whom some affinity is discovered. Love seeks the welfare of all and works no ill to any. Love seeks opportunity:

> "Therefore, as we have opportunity, let us do good to all, especially to those who are of the household of faith." (Galatians 6:10 NKJV)

In Summary:

- God the Father loves Jesus, God the Son,
- God's love expresses the deep, constant interest of a perfect God towards sinful people who are entirely unworthy,
- God's love produces and fosters a reverential "love" in the believer towards God Himself,
- God's love produces a practical "love" in believers towards others,
- God's love produces a desire to walk with Jesus and to obey God's commandments.

Question 6: Which aspect of God's love is important to you right now?

_____

_____

_____

_____

_____

Illustration: an example of God's love in the Old Testament that reflects the Gospel.

> "You search the Scriptures, for in them you think you have eternal life; and these are they which testify of Me." (John 5:39 NKJV)

We see a foreshadowing of the Gospel in the life of Joseph. We see glimpses of Jesus and the Gospel in the story of Joseph. (Genesis 37-50)

Here is a summary of Joseph's life and some of the parallels that I see pointing to Jesus.

His father, Jacob, loves Joseph. (Jacob gave a special coat to set him apart from his brothers – at Jesus' baptism, He was set apart from others. *"This is my beloved, whom I am well pleased."* Matthew 3:17) But Joseph was hated by his brothers. (Genesis 37:1-4) Joseph has his dreams that all would bow down to him. (Genesis 37:5-11) Then his brothers plot to kill him but instead sold him into slavery for 20 pieces of silver. (Genesis 37:12-36) Do you see any parallels?

Joseph lives an honorable life - fleeing temptations but is falsely accused and tossed into prison. (Genesis 39:1-23) There in prison, Joseph sits between two prisoners who both had dreams. Joseph interpreted the dreams, and one was executed, and the other was restored to his position in serving the Pharaoh according to the dream. Joseph told that restored prisoner: "Get me out of here!" (Genesis 40:1-23). Jesus died between two thieves; one was executed; the other was restored to live with Jesus.

Two years later, Pharaoh has two dreams, and Joseph interprets the dreams of the coming famine and is exalted to second in command over Egypt at the age of 30. (Genesis 41:1-57) Jesus rose from the grave to sit at the right hand of the Father. So, Joseph came out of his "tomb of death" and rose to power next to Pharaoh.

During the famine, Jacob sends his ten sons to Egypt to buy grain. (Genesis 42-44). At first, Joseph did not "reveal" himself and showed kindness and love instead of judgment. Jesus, before revealing Himself to us – showed us kindness (and no judgment). We did not deserve that kindness.

Joseph loved his brothers – even though they were undeserving. *"You meant it for evil; God meant it for good."* Genesis 50:20-21 (Genesis 45-50). Jesus prayed: "Father, forgive them – they do not know what they are doing." (Luke 23:34)

God used Joseph to save his brothers and the pagan Egyptians.

Question 7: How do you see the Gospel of Jesus' death, burial, and resurrection in Joseph's life in Genesis 37-50?

_____

_____

_____

_____

_____

Question 8: How does the story of Joseph and his brothers demonstrate this idea of love?

_____

_____

_____

_____

Application: Finding love at the Cross

Love had its perfect expression in the Lord Jesus Christ.

> *"For the love of Christ compels us, because we judge thus: that if One died for all, then all died; (15) and He died for all, that those who live should live no longer for themselves, but for Him who died for them and rose again." (2 Corinthians 5:14-15 NKJV)*

This love is wrapped in the Gospel – Paul always made the Gospel the central point in his teachings.

"But God, who is rich in mercy, because of His great love with which He loved us, (5) even when we were dead in trespasses, made us alive together with Christ (by grace you have been saved), (6) and raised us up together, and made us sit together in the heavenly places in Christ Jesus," (Ephesians 2:4-6 NKJV)

Our sins have been crucified on the Cross through Jesus – we were buried with Him – and made alive by the resurrection. Even now, we are at the right hand of the Father in Christ.

Question 9: How did Jesus show us His love for the believer from the verses above?

_____

_____

_____

_____

_____

Jesus kept pointing the disciples to the Cross as an explanation of His love for them.
John 10:1-30

The Good Shepherd is laying down His life for the sheep. As we come to the Cross – we see what love looks like. A bloody Savior was dying and carrying upon Himself our sins. And the proof that the sacrifice was effectual – the third day, Jesus rose from the dead.
John 13:1-17

While in the upper room on that last night before His crucifixion, Jesus left from the head of the table, stooped to wash the disciple's feet like an ordinary servant. Then returning to the head of the table. A picture of Jesus coming from heaven, to wash us clean at the Cross, and rising from the dead to return to the rightful place in heaven.
John 13:31-35

> *"A new commandment I give to you, that you love one another;
> as I have loved you, that you also love one another. (35) "By this,
> all will know that you are My disciples, if you have love for one
> another." (John 13:34-35 NKJV)*

Jesus told the disciples that they are to love in the same way He loves them – still not comprehending because Jesus had not yet gone to the Cross and rose from the dead three days later.

> *"This is My commandment, that you love one another as I have
> loved you. (13) "Greater love has no one than this, than to lay
> down one's life for his friends. (14) "You are My friends if you do
> whatever I command you." (John 15:12-14 NKJV)*

The Good Shepherd was laying down His life for the sheep. As we come to the Cross – we see what love looks like. A bloody Savior – One who was whipped until His back was like hamburger. He was mocked with a crown of thorns, then beaten while blindfolded. "Who hit You?" Jesus carried His Cross to Calvary, stripped of His clothing. Then nails were pounded into His hands and feet. He was lifted up on the Cross to bleed out – disfigured beyond recognition. For six hours on that Cross, He was dying and carrying upon Himself our sins. Jesus carried our sins into eternity as the Father judged Him. Jesus cried out, "My God, My God, why have You forsaken Me?" Jesus' last words, "It is finished." And He died. He was buried. And the proof that the sacrifice was effectual – the third day, Jesus rose from the dead.

That aspect of the Fruit of the Spirit of love is best seen in our lives as we look to imitate Jesus in His love for us.

> *Therefore, be imitators of God as dear children. (2) And walk
> in love, as Christ also has loved us and given Himself for us,
> an offering and a sacrifice to God for a sweet-smelling aroma.
> (Ephesians 5:1-2 NKJV)*

Question 10: According to the Bible, what does love look like?

Question 11: Pick one of the following questions and respond.
- How have you seen your sins crucified on the Cross?
- How does that love of God that was poured out upon you bring a heart of love in you?
- How has the blood become precious, and it causes you to love God and a desire to obey Him?
- How has the precious blood caused you to love your fellow believer and have a desire to be in sweet fellowship with them?

Joy

The fruit of the Spirit in Galatians 5:22-23 is the context of the battle going on within the Christian. Galatians 5:16-18:

> *"I say then: Walk in the Spirit, and you shall not fulfill the lust of the flesh. (17) For the flesh lusts against the Spirit, and the Spirit against the flesh; and these are contrary to one another, so that you do not do the things that you wish. (18) But if you are led by the Spirit, you are not under the law."*

... Paul gives a list of the works of the flesh then says, BUT….

> *"But the fruit of the Spirit is love, joy, peace, longsuffering, kindness, goodness, faithfulness, (23) gentleness, self-control. Against such there is no law." (Galatians 5:16-18, 22-23 NKJV)*

And Paul brings the discussion back to the Gospel, back to the Cross:

> *"And those who are Christ's have crucified the flesh with its passions and desires. (25) If we live in the Spirit, let us also walk in the Spirit. (26) Let us not become conceited, provoking one another, envying one another." (Galatians 5:24-26 NKJV)*

Walking in the Spirit in Joy
We are going to look at three things:

- Going to define joy and see some verses using joy
- Look at an example of joy from the Old Testament that reflects the Gospel.
- And showing how the Cross demonstrates joy.

Let's look at the second quality of the Fruit of the Spirit: Joy

What is joy?
Definition from the Greek word:
χαρά chará, joy, gladness; the joy received from you; the cause or occasion of joy; of persons who are one's joy Joyfulness, Joyfully, Joyous:

The thesaurus uses words like:

delight, pleasure, enjoyment, bliss, ecstasy, elation, joyfulness, thrill, gladness, exultation, rapture

Opposite words – grief, sadness, sorrow

Few examples of how the word "joy" is used:

To the shepherds at Jesus' birth:

> *"Then the angel said to them, "Do not be afraid, for behold, I bring you good tidings of great joy which will be to all people." (Luke 2:10 NKJV)*

The Magi saw the star looking for the King of the Jews:

> *"When they saw the star, they rejoiced with exceedingly great joy." (Matthew 2:10 NKJV)*

Question 1: Why do you think there was this joy at Jesus' birth?

When a person repents and believes the Gospel: Jesus' death, burial, and resurrection:

> *"I say to you that likewise there will be more joy in heaven over one sinner who repents than over ninety-nine just persons who need no repentance. ... (10) "Likewise, I say to you, there is joy in the presence of the angels of God over one sinner who repents."* (Luke 15:7, 10 NKJV)

Question 2: How is joy described when a person becomes a Christian when they believe? Why?

_____

_____

_____

_____

_____

(Concerning the coming events that will be happening – even when they did not understand yet),

> *"Most assuredly, I say to you that you will weep and lament, but the world will rejoice; and you will be sorrowful, but your sorrow will be turned into joy. (21) "A woman, when she is in labor, has sorrow because her hour has come; but as soon as she has given birth to the child, she no longer remembers the anguish, for joy that a human being has been born into the world. (22) "Therefore you now have sorrow; but I will see you again and your heart will rejoice, and your joy no one will take from you."* (John 16:20-22 NKJV)

Question 3: How is joy contrasted between the world and the disciples concerning the Cross and the resurrection?

After the resurrection and the Gospel's proclamation, we find joy starting to spread in the Church.
The disciples after Jesus' ascension:

> *"And they worshiped Him, and returned to Jerusalem with great joy" (Luke 24:52 NKJV)*

The results of Peter's preaching in Acts 2 and the joy of the people:

> *"So continuing daily with one accord in the temple, and breaking bread from house to house, they ate their food with gladness and simplicity of heart, (47) praising God and having favor with all the people. And the Lord added to the Church daily those who were being saved." (Acts 2:46-47 NKJV)*

Philip preaches Christ in Samaria,

> *"And there was great joy in that city." (Acts 8:8 NKJV)*

The results of Paul and Barnabas preaching to the Gentiles in Antioch

> *"And the disciples were filled with joy and with the Holy Spirit." (Acts 13:52 NKJV)*

Paul and Barnabas heading to Jerusalem for the first General Assembly to discuss if circumcision and keeping the law of Moses was necessary for salvation:

> *"So, being sent on their way by the Church, they passed through Phoenicia and Samaria, describing the conversion of the Gentiles; and they caused great joy to all the brethren." (Acts 15:3 NKJV)*

Question 4: Why all this joy within the early Church?
- ☐ There were great times of eating together (potlucks).
- ☐ The preaching of the Gospel was changing lives
- ☐ The preacher was doing his job and reaching people for Jesus.

As we read our Bibles, we will find many examples of joy and the application of that joy in our daily lives.
Do not use your Christian liberties to offend a brother in Christ.

> *"For the kingdom of God is not eating and drinking, but righteousness and peace and joy in the Holy Spirit." (Romans 14:17 NKJV)*

One of Paul's final instructions to the Church:

> *"Now may the God of hope fill you with all joy and peace in believing, that you may abound in hope by the power of the Holy Spirit." (Romans 15:13 NKJV)*

Paul in the context of preaching the Gospel to the believers in Philippi

> *"And being confident of this, I know that I shall remain and continue with you all for your progress and joy of faith." (Philippians 1:25 NKJV)*

Paul encourages the Church under persecution:

"And you became followers of us and of the Lord, having received the word in much affliction, with joy of the Holy Spirit." (1 Thessalonians 1:6 NKJV)

Then later, Paul says to the Church:

"For you are our glory and joy." (1 Thessalonians 2:20 NKJV)

"Obey those who rule over you, and be submissive, for they watch out for your souls, as those who must give account. Let them do so with joy and not with grief, for that would be unprofitable for you." (Hebrews 13:17 NKJV)

This joy comes as we believe the Gospel (Jesus' death, burial, and resurrection). Peter says:

"Whom having not seen you love. Though now you do not see Him, yet believing, you rejoice with joy inexpressible and full of glory." (1 Peter 1:8 NKJV)

And Peter goes on later to say this joy is found in Christ's sufferings:

"But rejoice to the extent that you partake of Christ's sufferings, that when His glory is revealed, you may also be glad with exceeding joy." (1 Peter 4:13 NKJV)

Question 5: How vital is joy within the life of the Church? What is the source of that joy?

_____

_____

_____

_____

_____

As you read the Psalms, there are many examples and exhortations for us to rejoice in the Lord.

> *"Be glad in the LORD and rejoice, you righteous; And shout for joy, all you upright in heart" (Psalm 32:11 NKJV)*

David's pray after confessing his sin:

> *"Restore to me the joy of Your salvation, And uphold me by Your generous Spirit." (Psalm 51:12 NKJV)*

Yes, we are to rejoice and be glad in the Lord. Even when we fall into sin, we can ask for the Lord to forgive us and restore the joy of the Lord's Salvation found there at the Cross.

Illustration: David's joy in returning the Ark to Jerusalem.
As we look at this account – I will be pointing out how we can see some shadows and types of Jesus and the Gospel in the passage. Jesus said we should see Him. John 5:39

David and the Ark. 2 Samuel 6 / 1 Chronicles 15

David has been established as King of Israel in Jerusalem (now called the City of David). The Ark was located in Baalah Judah / Kiriath-Jearim. (A city on the northern border of Judah and southern Benjamin near the western edge of the mountains of Judah, 9 to 10 miles from Jerusalem)

Philistines captured and then returned Ark – 1 Sam 6:21 and remained there for 20 years 1 Sam 7:1-2/ 1 Chron 13:5-6

God had laid it upon David's heart to bring the Ark to Jerusalem.

The Ark of God – whose name is called by "The name, the Lord of Hosts, who dwells between the cherubim." The Ark represented the very presence of God. (2 Samuel 6:2; 1 Chronicles 13:6)

Like Jesus was the very presence of God. Oh, how the Lord Jesus was zealous for Father and the temple (the location of the Ark)

> *"When He had made a whip of cords, He drove them all out of the temple, with the sheep and the oxen, and poured out the changers' money and overturned the tables. (16) And He said to those who sold doves, "Take these things away! Do not make My Father's house a house of merchandise!" (17) Then His disciples remembered that it was written, "Zeal for Your house has eaten Me up." (John 2:15-17 NKJV)*

David builds a tent – tabernacle in Jerusalem and retrieves the Ark – with 30,000 men, with much joy and celebration: two sons of Abinadab, a Levite, Uzzah, and Ahio, accompanied the Ark on a cart. I get the picture of Ahio on the front and Uzzah on the back. The Ark is in between two men - Oops: the wrong way to do this - Uzzah touches the Ark and dies. (2 Samuel 6: 1-11; 1 Chronicles 13:5-8)

Like the Ark (Jesus on the Cross - the presence of the Lord) – between two men – one dies the other lives.

David is now fearful of God and the Ark, and it stayed with Obed-Edom inside his house for three months. Not sure how far away this was from Jerusalem.

The Ark, after three months, comes out and returns to its rightful place in the tabernacle. A picture of the resurrection and Jesus returning to heaven.

David follows God's way – Levites carry the Ark on poles (2 Sam 6:12-16; 1 Chron 15:1-29). These poles were made of acacia wood overlaid with gold. *(Exodus 25:13-15)* As the wooden poles lifted up the Ark, so Jesus was also lifted up on a wooden Cross - not covered with gold – but something more precious – covered in His blood.

David is leaping and dancing with joy before the Lord. Every six paces sacrificed oxen and fatted sheep (2 Samuel 6:13) (that was a bloody trail). So was the trail of blood of Jesus' carrying His Cross from Jerusalem to outside the city – bleeding a trail of blood to Calvary.

Question 6: How do you respond to seeing these shadows and types of Jesus and the Gospel?

Oh, the joy of David as he danced leaping and whirling before the Lord with all his might. (2 Samuel 6:14)

> *"So, David, the elders of Israel, and the captains over thousands went to bring up the Ark of the covenant of the LORD from the house of Obed-Edom with joy. (26) And so it was, when God helped the Levites who bore the Ark of the covenant of the LORD, that they offered seven bulls and seven rams. (27) David was clothed with a robe of fine linen, as were all the Levites who bore the Ark, the singers, and Chenaniah the music master with the singers. David also wore a linen ephod. (28) Thus all Israel brought up the Ark of the covenant of the LORD with shouting and with the sound of the horn, with trumpets and with cymbals, making music with stringed instruments and harps." (1 Chronicles 15:25-28)*

This was quite a parade of joy as people are shouting, with a marching band.

Question 7: Do you find this type of joy when you come before the Cross and remind yourself of all the benefits found here in the Gospel?

_____

_____

_____

_____

_____

Then watch what happens.

When David finished offering the burnt and peace offerings, he blessed the people – then distributed among all the people, the whole multitude, both men and women – a loaf of bread, piece of meat, cake of raisins (Sam 6; 1 Chron 16:1-3; 2 Sam 6:17-19).

Then David wrote this Psalm: 1 Chron 16:7-36. Read this Psalm with the understanding that the Lord Jesus has entered into His glory as the Ark has entered into the tent. Read this Psalm in the light of the Gospel.

Question 8: Do you see Jesus in this Psalm of David? List the things you see we are to be doing considering the Cross.

_____

_____

_____

_____

_____

With a heart of joy and praise for the Lord, David comes home to bless his house (2 Samuel 6:21-23 / 1 Chronicles 16:43).

Earlier when David came into the city we read:

> *"And it happened, as the Ark of the covenant of the LORD came to the City of David, that Michal, Saul's daughter, looked through a window and saw King David whirling and playing music; and she despised him in her heart." [she was not celebrating with her husband] (2 Samuel 6:16; 1 Chronicles 15:29)*

> *"Then David returned to bless his household. And Michal the daughter of Saul came out to meet David, and (out of the abundance of the heart that now despised David) said, "How glorious was the king of Israel today, uncovering himself today in the eyes of the maids of his servants, as one of the base fellows shamelessly uncovers himself!" (21) So David said to Michal, "It was before the LORD, who chose me instead of your father and all his house, to appoint me ruler over the people of the LORD, over Israel. Therefore I will play music before the LORD. (22) "And I will be even more undignified than this, and will be humble in my own sight. But as for the maidservants of whom you have spoken, by them, I will be held in honor." (2 Samuel 6:20-22 NKJV)*

David did not allow the unjust criticism and exaggerations of Michal's bitterness to turn his joy and duty before the Lord. David had removed his royal robes and was rejoicing in humility with the rest of the singers, and not as some "important king" before the Lord.

The Lord brought shame and judgment upon Michal:

> *"Therefore Michal, the daughter of Saul, had no children to the day of her death." (2 Samuel 6:20-23 NKJV)*

Question 9: Have you ever "looked down" on others in their worship of the Lord? Have you despised others for their joy that you are not able or want to join? Be careful – the Lord could cause you to be barren.

Application: Let's return to the Cross and see the joy that is offered.

> *"Therefore my heart is glad, and my glory rejoices; My flesh also will rest in hope. (10) For You will not leave my soul in Sheol, Nor will You allow Your Holy One to see corruption. (11) You will show me the path of life; In Your presence is fullness of joy; At Your right hand are pleasures." (Psalm 16:9-11 NKJV)*

Do you know who is speaking in this Psalm? It says at the beginning that this Psalm is a Michtam of David. But I would like us to look at this Psalm from Jesus' perspective.

Let's look at these verses again: Jesus is praying:

> *"Therefore, my heart is glad, and my glory rejoices; My flesh also will rest in hope. (10) For You (Father) will not leave my soul in Sheol, Nor will You allow Your Holy One (Jesus) to see corruption.*

Though Jesus experienced death and hell for us – He knew that He would raise from the tomb on the third day.

> *(11) You (Father) will show me the path of life; In Your presence is fullness of joy; At Your right hand are pleasures (Psalm 16:9-11 NKJV)*

Forty days after the resurrection – Jesus ascended up into the clouds – to take His rightful place AGAIN at the right hand of the Father."

(by the way – Peter did this with the Psalm in his first sermon in Acts 2:14-39)

Question 10: How do you see the joy that Jesus is looking forward to when He returns to heaven after His resurrection from Psalm 16?

That is why when we read Hebrews 12 – we see Jesus going to the Cross with the joy that was set before Him.

The joy set before Jesus while enduring the Cross.

> *"Therefore we also, since we are surrounded by so great a cloud of witnesses, let us lay aside every weight, and the sin which so easily ensnares us, and let us run with endurance the race that is set before us, (2) looking unto Jesus, the author and finisher of our faith, who for the joy that was set before Him endured the cross, despising the shame, and has sat down at the right hand of the throne of God. (3) For consider Him who endured such hostility from sinners against Himself, lest you become weary and discouraged in your souls. (4) You have not yet resisted to bloodshed, striving against sin." (Hebrews 12:1-4 NKJV)*

Question 11: Jesus went to the Cross with joy. Why?

_____

_____

_____

_____

_____

Have you taken time to consider Jesus' passion?
Hebrews 12:3 says to Consider: ἀναλογίζομαι analogízomai to think over, ponder, to consider by weighing, comparing

Consider Him:

Consider Him: at the Last Supper

John 13 – washed feet.

Institutes the Lord's Supper **Matthew 26, Mark 14, Luke 22** – Do this in remembrance – (i.e., consider Him) Take, eat, this is my body, this cup is the new covenant in My blood, which is shed for you.

Consider Him: On the way to the Garden

John 15:9-11 – I have loved you; I will lay down my life

> _"These things I have spoken to you, that My joy may remain in you, and that your joy may be full." (John 15:11 NKJV)_

The sorrow of Jesus' death will turn into joy:

> _"Most assuredly, I say to you that you will weep and lament, but the world will rejoice; and you will be sorrowful, but your sorrow will be turned into joy." (John 16:20 NKJV)_

Consider Him: in the Garden prayer

Matthew 26:36-46, Mark 14:32-42, Luke 22:39-46:

"Then He said to them, "My soul is exceedingly sorrowful, even to death. Stay here and watch with Me." (39) He went a little farther and fell on His face, and prayed, saying, "O My Father, if it is possible, let this cup pass from Me; nevertheless, not as I will, but as You will." (Matthew 26:38-39 NKJV)

"Jesus spoke these words, lifted up His eyes to heaven, and said: "Father, the hour has come. Glorify Your Son, that Your Son also may glorify You, ... (13) "But now I come to You, and these things I speak in the world, that they may have My joy fulfilled in themselves." (John 17:1, 13 NKJV)

Consider Him: being Arrested and betrayed (Judas and Peter)

Judas sells Jesus for 30 pieces of silver and leads a mob to arrest Jesus. (Matthew 26:47-56; Mark 14:43-52; Luke 47-53; John 18:1-11)

Peter denies Jesus. (Matthew 26:69-75; Mark 14:66-72; Luke 22:54-62; John 18:15-27)

Question 12: As you consider these events above, what stands out for you?

_____

_____

_____

_____

_____

Consider Him: with False charges, false witnesses.

Before Pilate (Matthew 27:1-14, Mark 15:1-5; Luke 23:1-5; John 18:28-38) Jews plot to kill Jesus and bring false accusations – Pilate finds no fault. Barabbas is released by being persuaded by the Jewish rulers.

Consider Him: His beatings, mockings, and humiliation.

Pilate had Jesus scourged – the soldiers mocked Jesus, crown of thorns, purple robe (Matthew 27:27-31; Mark 15:16-20, John 19:5-19)

"Crucify Him, crucify Him" (Matthew 27:22-25; Mark 15:10-15; Luke 23:20-25; John 19:5-16)

Consider Him: Carrying a Cross and being crucified

Jesus carries His Cross [with Simon a Cyrenian] between two thieves – Soldiers divided His garments and cast lots (Matthew 27:32-35; Mark 15:21-24; Luke 23:26-33; John 19:17-18)

Consider Him: others Mocking – wagging their heads, blasphemed Him.

By the Pharisees, scribes, and elders, and thieves:

> *"He saved others, let Him save Himself – IF HE IS THE CHRIST – then we will believe." (Matthew 27:39-44; Mark 15:29-32; Luke 23:35-39)*

Question 13: As you consider the above, what stands out for you?

_____

_____

_____

_____

_____

Consider Him: Becoming sin

> *"For He made Him who knew no sin to be sin for us, that we might become the righteousness of God in Him." (2 Corinthians 5:21 NKJV)*

> *"Surely He has borne our griefs And carried our sorrows; Yet we esteemed Him stricken, Smitten by God, and afflicted. (5) But He was wounded for our transgressions, He was bruised*

for our iniquities; The chastisement for our peace was upon Him, And by His stripes we are healed. (6) All we like sheep have gone astray; We have turned, everyone, to his own way; And the LORD has laid on Him the iniquity of us all." (Isaiah 53:4-6 NKJV)

"Christ has redeemed us from the curse of the law, having become a curse for us (for it is written, "Cursed is everyone who hangs on a tree"). (Galatians 3:13 NKJV)

"For Christ also suffered once for sins, the just for the unjust, that He might bring us to God, being put to death in the flesh but made alive by the Spirit." (1 Peter 3:18 NKJV)

Consider Him: His prayers from the Cross

"Father forgive them, for they do not know what they do." (Luke 23:34)

"My God, My God, why have You forsaken Me?" (Matthew 27:46; Mark 15:34)

"I thirst!" (John 19:28)

"It is finished!" (John 19:30)

"Father, into Your hands I commit My spirit." (Luke 23:46)

Consider Him: His death
Jesus cried out with a loud voice and died: (Matthew 27:50-56; Mark 15:37-41; Luke 23:46-49; John 19:30) Soldier pierced His side and out flowed water and blood, and the Centurion said: *"Truly this was the Son of God."*

Consider Him: His burial
Joseph of Arimathea with Nicodemus buried in his tomb. (Matthew 27:57-66; Mark 15:42-47; Luke 23:50-56; John 19:38-42)

Wrapped body, placed in the tomb, rolled a stone – the Pharisees set a guard. Witnesses saw the burial site

Consider Him: His resurrection

The stone is rolled away. (Matthew 28:1-10; Mark 16:1-13; Luke 24:1-49; John 20:1-18-31; 1 Corinthians 15:5-8)

The tomb is empty; Angles say: He is not here; He has risen - Mary sees Jesus first; Jesus' first words: *"Rejoice!"* The disciples on the road to Emmaus, Jesus explains all the Old Testament pointed to Him. Appears to disciples, to Thomas the next week. Explains the Old Testament. Jesus is seen for the next 40 days by the women, Peter, the disciples, over 500 at once, by James (Jesus' bio brother), Paul.

Consider Him: His ascension (Mark 16:19; Luke 24:50-53; Acts 1:9)

After giving the disciples the charge of the great commission, Jesus ascends into heaven before their eyes.

Question 14: As you consider the above points, what stands out for you?

_____

_____

_____

_____

_____

Yes, as we come to the Cross and stop, look up, we are filled with joy and gratitude. Those thoughts of discouragement are seen in the perspective that the world is unable to understand. Even Jesus has a sense of joy as He went to the Cross. (Hebrews 12:1-3). Why? Because He was looking past the Cross, past the tomb, and even past the resurrection. He was looking ahead to the time when all would be united in glory with Him. That day when every believer will see Him face to face.

"Whom having not seen you love. Though now you do not see Him, yet believing, you rejoice with joy inexpressible and full of glory" (1 Peter 1:8 NKJV)

"Beloved, now we are children of God; and it has not yet been revealed what we shall be, but we know that when He is revealed, we shall be like Him, for we shall see Him as He is." (1 John 3:2 NKJV)

This is why James can say:

"My brethren, count it all joy when you fall into various trials." (James 1:2 NKJV)

The same joy that Jesus had going to the Cross – We also have that same joy – we can suffer with joy. Why? Because we look past the suffering to the fact that we will be with Jesus. We will enjoy and experience all the benefits of being a child of God – with no more pain, no more tears.

"These things I have spoken to you, that My joy may remain in you, and that your joy may be full." (John 15:11 NKJV)

"Most assuredly, I say to you that you will weep and lament, but the world will rejoice; and you will be sorrowful, but your sorrow will be turned into joy. (21) "A woman, when she is in labor, has sorrow because her hour has come; but as soon as she has given birth to the child, she no longer remembers the anguish, for joy that a human being has been born into the world. (22) "Therefore you now have sorrow; but I will see you again and your heart will rejoice, and your joy no one will take from you." (John 16:20-22 NKJV)

"But let all those rejoice who put their trust in You; Let them ever shout for joy, because You defend them; Let those also who love Your name Be joyful in You." (Psalm 5:11 NKJV)

"Restore to me the joy of Your salvation, And uphold me by Your generous Spirit." (Psalm 51:12 NKJV)

Question 15: How are you experiencing the joy of the Lord as you come to the Cross and consider Him?

Peace

$\mathcal{T}$he context of the fruit of the Spirit in Galatians 5:22-23 is the battle going on within the Christian.

> *"I say then: Walk in the Spirit, and you shall not fulfill the lust of the flesh. (17) For the flesh lusts against the Spirit, and the Spirit against the flesh; and these are contrary to one another, so that you do not do the things that you wish. (18) But if you are led by the Spirit, you are not under the law."* **Galatians 5:16-18**

Paul gives a list of the works of the flesh (Galatians 5:19-20) then says, BUT….

> *"But the fruit of the Spirit is love, joy, peace, longsuffering, kindness, goodness, faithfulness, (23) gentleness, self-control. Against such there is no law." (Galatians 22-23 NKJV)*

And Paul brings the discussion back to the Gospel, back to the Cross:

> *"And those who are Christ's have crucified the flesh with its passions and desires. (25) If we live in the Spirit, let us also walk in the Spirit." (Galatians 5:24-25 NKJV)*

The only way to see the fruit of the Spirit in your life – is by coming to the Cross. Let's look at the third quality of the Fruit of the Spirit: Peace.

Walking in the Spirit in Peace
We are going to look at three things in this lesson:

- Going to define peace and look at some verses using peace
- Look at an example of peace from the Old Testament that reflects the Gospel.
- And show how the Cross demonstrates peace.

Let's look at the third quality of the Fruit of the Spirit: Peace

What is Peace?

Definition from the Greek word:

εἰρήνη **eirḗnē, i-ray'-nay**; peace (literally or figuratively); a quietness, rest, a state of tranquility, freedom from the rage and havoc of war, peace between individuals and within a community, i.e., harmony, safety, happiness

Considering our peace with God: it is the tranquil state of a soul assured of its salvation through Christ. We fear nothing from God and are content with our earthly lot, as well as after death.

Few examples of how the word "peace" is used:

There are 4 uses of peace between others.

1. **THE PEACEFUL RELATIONSHIP BETWEEN GOD AND THE CHRISTIAN, ACCOMPLISHED THROUGH THE GOSPEL – JESUS' DEATH, BURIAL, AND RESURRECTION.**

Jesus was preparing the disciples for His death and reassured them that in Him, there is peace:

"Peace I leave with you, My peace I give to you; not as the world gives do I give to you. Let not your heart be troubled, neither let it be afraid." (John 14:27 NKJV)

"These things I have spoken to you, that in Me you may have peace. In the world you will have tribulation; but be of good cheer, I have overcome the world." (John 16:33 NKJV)

Paul reminds us that we are at peace with God by faith through our Lord Jesus Christ because Christ died for us.

"Therefore, having been justified by faith, we have peace with God through our Lord Jesus Christ... (6) For when we were still without strength, in due time, Christ died for the ungodly." (Romans 5:1, 6 NKJV)

"But now in Christ Jesus, you who once were far off have been brought near by the blood of Christ. (14) For He Himself is our peace, who has made both one, and has broken down the middle wall of separation, [speaking of the separation between Jews and Gentiles] (15) having abolished in His flesh the enmity, that is, the law of commandments contained in ordinances, so as to create in Himself one new man from the two, thus making peace, (16) and that He might reconcile them both to God in one body through the Cross, thereby putting to death the enmity. (17) And He came and preached peace to you who were afar off and to those who were near. (18) For through Him, we both have access by one Spirit to the Father." (Ephesians 2:13-18 NKJV)

Notice how Paul views the peace we have because of the Gospel. Jesus has brought us near, by the blood to the Father; Jesus is our peace. Jesus has reconciled us to God the Father through the Cross

"and the peace of God, which surpasses all understanding, will guard your hearts and minds through Christ Jesus." (Philippians 4:7 NKJV)

When we consider this "peace of God," it surpassed all human understanding that the world cannot comprehend.

"and by Him to reconcile all things to Himself, by Him, whether things on earth or things in heaven, having made peace through the blood of His Cross." (Colossians 1:20 NKJV)

It is through a bloody Cross we are reconciled to God. It is through a bloody Cross that we will find peace.

Question 1: Have you truly found peace with God? Have you found peace through this bloody Cross? Share a brief testimony of how you found this peace.

_____

_____

_____

_____

_____

2. BECAUSE OF THE GOSPEL, WE OUGHT TO STRIVE FOR PEACEFUL RELATIONSHIPS WITH ALL PEOPLE:

Jesus said on the Sermon on the mount:

> *"Blessed are the peacemakers, For they shall be called sons of God."
> (Matthew 5:9 NKJV)*

Paul encouraged the believer to be at peace with all people:

> *"Therefore do not let your good be spoken of as evil; (17) for the kingdom of God is not eating and drinking, but righteousness and peace and joy in the Holy Spirit. (18) For he who serves Christ in these things is acceptable to God and approved by men. (19) Therefore let us pursue the things which make for peace and the things by which one may edify another." (Romans 14:16-19 NKJV)*

> *"If it is possible, as much as depends on you, live peaceably with all men." (Romans 12:18 NKJV)*

Question 2: How is your relationship with the people around you? Do you have the reputation of being a peacemaker?

_____

_____

_____

_____

_____

3. PEACE COMES WITH THE RIGHT APPLICATION OF THE GOSPEL WITHIN THE CHURCH.

Notice how often Paul speaks about the importance of peace within the body of Christ – the church.

> _"endeavoring to keep the unity of the Spirit in the bond of peace. (4) There is one body and one Spirit, just as you were called in one hope of your calling; (5) one Lord, one faith, one baptism; (6) one God and Father of all, who is above all, and through all, and in you all. (7) But to each one of us grace was given according to the measure of Christ's gift." (Ephesians 4:3-7 NKJV)_

> _"For God is not the author of confusion but of peace, as in all the churches of the saints." (1 Corinthians 14:33 NKJV)_

> _"Now the God of peace be with you all. Amen." (Romans 15:33 NKJV)_

> _"Now may the Lord of peace Himself give you peace always in every way. The Lord be with you all." (2 Thessalonians 3:16 NKJV)_

"Now may the God of peace who brought up our Lord Jesus from the dead, that great Shepherd of the sheep, through the blood of the everlasting covenant, make you complete in every good work to do His will, working in you what is well pleasing in His sight, through Jesus Christ, to whom be glory forever and ever. Amen."
Hebrews 13:20-21 (NKJV)

There ought to be peace in the church at all times.

Question 3: Have you ever been in or heard of a church where there was "no peace?" Why was there no peace?

The Scriptures are clear if we find no peace in the Church:

> *"If a wise man contends with a foolish man, Whether the fool rages or laughs, there is no peace." (Proverbs 29:9 NKJV)*

It is possible to have foolish people within the church. Even the wise man is unable to contend because the fool will not listen.

> *"There is no peace," says the LORD, "for the wicked." (Isaiah 48:22 NKJV)*

The fool has no peace – because there is still wickedness controlling the heart: *("I say then: Walk in the Spirit, and you shall not fulfill the lust of the flesh."*

Galatians 5:16 (NKJV) Look at that list of the works of the flesh that pertain to no peace:

> *"Now the works of the flesh are evident, which are: adultery, fornication, uncleanness, lewdness, idolatry, sorcery, hatred, contentions, jealousies, outbursts of wrath, selfish ambitions, dissensions, heresies, envy, murders, drunkenness, revelries, and the like; of which I tell you beforehand, just as I also told you in time past, that those who practice such things will not inherit the kingdom of God." Galatians 5:19-21 (NKJV)*

Question 4: Why do you think people are like this within the Church?

_____

_____

_____

_____

_____

They have **NOT** come to the Cross for reconciliation; they are **NOT** crucified with Christ and are **NOT** walking in the Spirit. Christians can do these things: Look at how this wickedness is expressed in Proverbs 6:

> *"These six things the LORD hates, Yes, seven are an abomination to Him: (17) A proud look, A lying tongue, Hands that shed innocent blood, (18) A heart that devises wicked plans, Feet that are swift in running to evil, (19) A false witness who speaks lies, And one who sows discord among brethren." (Proverbs 6:16-19 NKJV)*

All of these seven things that are an abomination to the Lord come from a sinful, self-centered, self-promoting, self-seeking heart that does not want to do things God's way:

"But if you have bitter envy and self-seeking in your hearts, do not boast and lie against the truth. (15) This wisdom does not descend from above, but is earthly, sensual, demonic. (16) For where envy and self-seeking exist, confusion and every evil thing are there." (James 3:14-16 NKJV)

James is clear – any confusion within the church is demonic in origin. And shows itself in being self-seeking. It is about ME.

Question 5: When there are confusion and dissension within the body of Christ, someone has become bitter, self-seeking, envious, and being used by demonic forces. What is the result of this type of confusion?

Question 6: Where do you find peace? How can there be peace within the Body?

4. THE GOSPEL CAN ALSO BRING PEACE BETWEEN NATIONS,

"Glory to God in the highest, And on earth peace, goodwill toward men!" (Luke 2:14 NKJV)

"To give light to those who sit in darkness and the shadow of death, To guide our feet into the way of peace." (Luke 1:79 NKJV)

I'm confident there will be world peace. But only after the final judgment and the re-creation of the new heavens and the new earth. Until then:

"If it is possible, as much as depends on you, live peaceably with all men." (Romans 12:18 NKJV)

Question 7: How are you doing in living in peace with all those around you?

_____

_____

_____

_____

_____

Illustration: Noah's Ark
Side note: There is "The Ark Encounter" in Williamstown, KY. I highly recommend you go with your family for a whole day of exploring the Ark. Also, in Branson at the Sight and Sound Theater – Noah – the musical – now playing.
   God was sorry that He had made man on earth:

"Then the LORD saw that the wickedness of man was great in the earth, and that every intent of the thoughts of his heart was only evil continually. (6) And the LORD was sorry that He had made

man on the earth, and He was grieved in His heart. (7) So the LORD said, "I will destroy man whom I have created from the face of the earth, both man and beast, creeping thing and birds of the air, for I am sorry that I have made them." (8) **BUT** *Noah found grace in the eyes of the LORD." (Genesis 6:5-8 NKJV)*

God gave a very specific job to Noah.:

"And God said to Noah, "The end of all flesh has come before Me, for the earth is filled with violence through them; and behold, I will destroy them with the earth. (14) "Make yourself an ark of gopherwood; make rooms in the ark, and cover it inside and outside with pitch. (15) "And this is how you shall make it: The length of the ark shall be three hundred cubits, its width fifty cubits, and its height thirty cubits. (16) "You shall make a window for the ark, and you shall finish it to a cubit from above; and set the door of the ark in its side. You shall make it with lower, second, and third decks. (17) "And behold, I Myself am bringing floodwaters on the earth, to destroy from under heaven all flesh in which is the breath of life; everything that is on the earth shall die. (18) "But I will establish My covenant with you; and you shall go into the ark--you, your sons, your wife, and your sons' wives with you. (19) "And of every living thing of all flesh, you shall bring two of every sort into the ark, to keep them alive with you; they shall be male and female. (20) "Of the birds after their kind, of animals after their kind, and of every creeping thing of the earth after its kind, two of every kind will come to you to keep them alive. (21) "And you shall take for yourself of all food that is eaten, and you shall gather it to yourself; and it shall be food for you and for them." (22) Thus Noah did; according to all that God commanded him, so he did." (Genesis 6:13-22 NKJV)

After Noah completed the Ark, they loaded the food and animals: it began to rain 40 days and 40 nights. The underground waters came breaking through. The water covered the mountains. ALL FLESH that breathed air DIED. The waters prevailed for 150 days.

Noah and his family are in the Ark. There is safety and peace inside the ark when the Lord brought judgment upon the whole earth. Noah may have gotten sea-sick – but they were safe and in God's peace.

Question 8: Did you see the Gospel in this flood story? Jesus' death, burial, and resurrection? Where?

_____

_____

_____

_____

_____

- The floods of judgment upon the Earth came killing all that had breath
- Earth buried in a watery tomb
- Earth resurrects from that watery tomb and brings life,

But wait – there is more! Let's go back and look at the Ark itself: I would like to show you another aspect of the Gospel.

Read Genesis 6:14 from different translations if you are able.

Look at verse 14. Notice the Hebrew words:

> *"Make yourself an ark of gopherwood; make rooms in the ark, and cover it [רָפַכ kâphar,] inside and outside with pitch. [רֶפֹכ kôpher]*
> *(Genesis 6:14 NKJV)*

Are you seeing the Gospel more clearly now? From this verse? Not yet?

[רָפַכ kâphar]. H3722 KJV – 1x pitch; NKJV – 1x cover

This particular word is used 102x in OT. It is translated: 71x atonement; 70% of the time

[רֶפֹכ kôpher]. H3724 KJV -1x pitch; NKJV – 1x pitch

This word is used 17x in OT. It is translated: 8x – ransom, 2x satisfaction, 59% of the time

Are you seeing the Gospel now?

Noah was safe and at peace inside the Ark – So we are safe there at the foot of the Cross, hiding in Christ's atonement. As God's judgment was being poured out on Christ – we are safe from the Father's wrath and judgment - being covered by the precious blood of the atonement.

Noah came out of the Ark into a new creation.

Question 9: How have you found safety and peace inside the Ark of atonement? When life gets rough – do you go to the Cross and find peace in the atoning blood of Christ? The blood is not just for salvation.

Application: Let's return to the Cross and see the peace that is offered.

"For unto us a Child is born, Unto us a Son is given; And the government will be upon His shoulder. And His name will be called Wonderful, Counselor, Mighty God, Everlasting Father, Prince of Peace. (7) Of the increase of His government and peace There will be no end, Upon the throne of David and over His kingdom, To order it and establish it with judgment and justice From that time forward, even forever. The zeal of the LORD of hosts will perform this." (Isaiah 9:6-7 NKJV)

Jesus came to complete and fulfill the Law of God.

"Do not think that I came to destroy the Law or the Prophets. I did not come to destroy but to fulfill." (Matthew 5:17 NKJV)

"then He said, "Behold, I have come to do Your will, O God." He takes away the first that He may establish the second. (10) By that will, we have been sanctified through the offering of the body of Jesus Christ once for all. (11) And every priest stands ministering daily and offering repeatedly the same sacrifices, which can never take away sins. (12) But this Man, after He had offered one sacrifice for sins forever, sat down at the right hand of God." (Hebrews 10:9-12 NKJV)

Question 10: How are you seeing Jesus being our "prince of peace?"

_____

_____

_____

_____

_____

Another one of the OT sacrifices that Jesus fulfilled was the peace offering. Let's quickly consider the Peace Offering in light of the Gospel.

Peace Offerings: are NOT sin offerings.

(Heb. shelamim), detailed regulations regarding this Peace offering are found in **Leviticus 3**; and **Leviticus 7**.

The Law of the Peace Offering:

The peace offerings indicated right relations with God, expressing good-fellowship, gratitude, and obligation. Jesus, when He came to the Cross – He was in good-fellowship with the Father. Jesus came in gratitude and obligation before the Father.

The peace offering was to be eaten by the person offering it and the priest that brought that offering to the altar. There they would eat that offering in fellowship with God and one another.

They were of three aspects or application of the peace offering,

- **The Peace Offering is a thanksgiving offering** - expressive of gratitude for blessings received.

Jesus gave thanks when He instituted the Lord's supper.

He gave thanks for the bread: *"This is My body – take and eat,"*

He gave thanks for the wine: *"this is My blood of the new covenant, drink all of it."*

(Matthew 26:26-30; Mark 14:22-26; Luke 22:14-23; 1 Corinthians 11:23-26)

- **The Peace Offering is in fulfillment of a vow**, but expressive also of thanks for benefits received

Jesus fulfilled His vow with the Father:

> *"I have glorified You on the earth. I have finished the work which You have given Me to do." (John 17:4 NKJV)*

- **The Peace Offering is a free-will offering**, something spontaneously devoted to God

Jesus gave Himself willingly to be our sacrifice for sin:

> *"He went a little farther and fell on His face, and prayed, saying, "O My Father, if it is possible, let this cup pass from Me; nevertheless, not as I will, but as You will." (Matthew 26:39 NKJV)*

Question 11: Jesus has become your _____ offering before the Father.

Jesus is your peace offering.
Are you seeing the fruit of the Spirit flowing from the Cross?

Are you seeing now that love, joy, and now peace flow from the Cross?

"Therefore, having been justified by faith, we have peace with God through our Lord Jesus Christ." (Romans 5:1 NKJV)

"Therefore, if anyone is in Christ, he is a new creation; old things have passed away; behold, all things have become new. (18) Now all things are of God, who has reconciled us to Himself through Jesus Christ, and has given us the ministry of reconciliation, (19) that is, that God was in Christ reconciling the world to Himself, not imputing their trespasses to them, and has committed to us the word of reconciliation. (20) Now then, we are ambassadors for Christ, as though God were pleading through us: we implore you on Christ's behalf, be reconciled to God. (21) For He made Him who knew no sin to be sin for us, that we might become the righteousness of God in Him." (2 Corinthians 5:17-21 NKJV)

We are God's ambassadors for Christ. You have been made a new creature in Christ. Are you imploring others to be reconciled, come into peaceful terms with God? Are you pointing to the Cross and showing others? – "There is our peace. Believe in Him." Are you inviting others to come and worship our Prince of Peace?

Question 12: What final thoughts do you have concerning the fruit of peace?

Longsuffering

*T*he context of the fruit of the Spirit in Galatians 5:22-23 is the battle going on within the Christian.

> *"I say then: Walk in the Spirit, and you shall not fulfill the lust of the flesh. (17) For the flesh lusts against the Spirit, and the Spirit against the flesh; and these are contrary to one another, so that you do not do the things that you wish. (18) But if you are led by the Spirit, you are not under the law." Galatians 5:16-18*

Paul gives a list of the works of the flesh (Galatians 5:19-20) then says, BUT….

> *"But the fruit of the Spirit is love, joy, peace, longsuffering, kindness, goodness, faithfulness, (23) gentleness, self-control. Against such there is no law." (Galatians 22-23 NKJV)*

And Paul brings the discussion back to the Gospel, back to the Cross:

> *"And those who are Christ's have crucified the flesh with its passions and desires. (25) If we live in the Spirit, let us also walk in the Spirit." (Galatians 5:24-25 NKJV)*

The only way to see the fruit of the Spirit in your life – is by coming to the Cross. Let's look at the Forth quality of the Fruit of the Spirit: Longsuffering.

Walking in the Spirit in Longsuffering

- How does the Bible use longsuffering?
- What illustration from the Old Testament shows longsuffering?
- How do we see from the Cross longsuffering?

What is Longsuffering?

Definition from the Greek word:

μακροθυμία makrothymía, mak-roth-oo-mee'-ah; from the same (makros, "long," thumos, "temper"), longsuffering, patience, endurance, constancy, steadfastness, perseverance, forbearance, slowness in avenging wrongs

Longsuffering means the power to bear up under a burden—a power to endure—a power to resist pressure—the capacity to stand a tremendous strain that comes only from living and walking in the Holy Spirit because we have crucified the flesh with its passions and desires. We come to the Cross to find that power.

Holy Spirit longsuffering is perhaps that power which enables us to suffer on, which will not let us become ruffled, or paralyzed, or overwhelmed by difficulties as they come upon us. This longsuffering is having godly patience while in the midst of suffering.

That longsuffering or patience, which is a part of the fruit of the Spirit, stands opposed to works of the flesh: hatred, contentions, jealousies, outbursts of wrath, selfish ambitions, dissensions, envy, revelries, irritability of temper, fretfulness under sufferings, and weariness in well-doing. Longsuffering does not hold a grudge.

Christian patience or longsuffering must be distinguished from the resilience of self-effort and stoic apathy.

We are not talking about being a "stoic," The philosopher Zeno (3rd century BC) was the master of this school of Stoics. He taught that men should be free from passion, unmoved by joy or grief and that they should submit without complaint to the unavoidable hardships of life by which, as he supposed, all things were governed.

The word "stoic" commonly refers to someone indifferent to pain, pleasure, grief, or joy. The modern usage as a "person who represses feelings or endures patiently"

Longsuffering is NOT being a stoic. Instead, it speaks of the steadfastness of the soul while being provoked, being deliberately egged on. Yet, the one who has been crucified with Christ patiently endures the wrong under ill-treatment, without anger or thought of revenge. In a spirit of forgiveness and love. The one walking in the Spirit will suffer a long time by the hands of others for THEIR sake.

Question 1: Have you experienced this type of Holy Spirit longsuffering? Or are you the "stoic" type that refuses to feel? Or are you the type that has no patience at all for anything or anyone that crosses your path? Take a moment and ask yourself – am I longsuffering? How did you answer?

Example of God's longsuffering toward people

> *"who formerly were disobedient, when once the Divine longsuffering waited in the days of Noah, while the ark was being prepared, in which a few, that is, eight souls, were saved through water." (1 Peter 3:20 NKJV)*

God's longsuffering (holding off His wrath) [120 years] resulted in Noah's salvation and his family.

> *"What if God, wanting to show His wrath and to make His power known, endured with much longsuffering the vessels of wrath prepared for destruction." (Romans 9:22 NKJV)*

God holds off His wrath and anger by being longsuffering toward others' wickedness – to make His power known.

> *"The Lord is not slack concerning His promise, as some count slackness, but is longsuffering toward us, not willing that any should perish but that all should come to repentance." (2 Peter 3:9 NKJV)*

God holds off bringing judgment so those who will believe will repent.

> *"For God so loved the world that He gave His only begotten Son, that whoever believes in Him should not perish but have everlasting life. (17) "For God did not send His Son into the world to condemn the world, but that the world through Him might be saved. (18) "He who believes in Him is not condemned; BUT he who does not believe is condemned already, because he has not believed in the name of the only begotten Son of God. ... (35) "The Father loves the Son, and has given all things into His hand. (36) "He who believes in the Son has everlasting life; and he who does not believe the Son shall not see life, but the wrath of God abides on him." (John 3:16-18, 35-36 NKJV)*

God loves all – and His longsuffering is seen as the Gospel is offered to all that will believe. But there is a day coming that those who do not believe will experience the wrath of God, and His longsuffering ends.

Question 2: How have you seen the Lord's longsuffering in waiting for you to trust and believe in Him? Not merely for your salvation, but in your growth and walk with Jesus?

"Or do you despise the riches of His goodness, forbearance, and longsuffering, not knowing that the goodness of God leads you to repentance? (5) But in accordance with your hardness and your impenitent heart you are treasuring up for yourself wrath in the day of wrath and revelation of the righteous judgment of God." (Romans 2:4-5 NKJV).

God's goodness leads to repentance – His longsuffering allows the message of the Gospel to continue before people.

"and consider that the longsuffering of our Lord is salvation -" (2 Peter 3:15a NKJV).

We will look at how Jesus' longsuffering brings us salvation later.

"However, for this reason I obtained mercy, that in me first Jesus Christ might show all longsuffering, as a pattern to those who are going to believe on Him for everlasting life." (1 Timothy 1:16 NKJV)

God's longsuffering to Paul shows the grace God gives to those who should have perished (Paul – the killer of Christians)

Question 3: Do you see the need to be longsuffering with others? How are you patiently sharing the Gospel with those who seem to have hearts of stone? Have you given up hope that they will ever repent?

How does the Christian show and demonstrate this Holy Spirit fruit of longsuffering?

How does the Spirit develop the capacity of longsuffering in the soul? How does He make man able to bear losses, disappointments, aggravations, griefs, and all the ills that the flesh endures?

We answer that the Spirit accomplishes this effect by teaching us the relative value of things in light of the Gospel and viewing Jesus from the Cross.

Longsuffering: is not so much a patient waiting for good things to come, for more grace, and glory, through the Spirit; [waiting in line to check out, waiting for a light to change, waiting for your number to be called to get your food, This is NOT longsuffering - but....

Longsuffering is patiently bearing and enduring present evils with joyfulness, being strengthened by the Spirit with all might, according to His glorious power found at the resurrection; being slow to anger, ready to forgive injuries, put up with insults, and bear with one another: which is usually accompanied with gentleness, humanity, friendliness, courteousness, shown both in words, gestures, and actions; in imitation of the gentleness of Christ and highlighted there on the Cross, living in the wisdom of that heavenly doctrine of the Gospel (Jesus' death, burial, and resurrection). *Longsuffering* is to defer anger and the ability to bear injuries.

Longsuffering. —is to moderate our anger and desire for revenge when many and great wrongs are done to us. Longsuffering is a demonstration of the power of the Gospel within the life of a Christian.

Question 4: Are you slow to anger? Have you forgiven others who have wronged you? Or do you still hold a grudge concerning others? How did you answer?

How is longsuffering exhibited in our lives?

1. **Longsuffering sees God's hand in affliction, and so is quieted under them.**

"And he said: "Naked I came from my mother's womb, And naked shall I return there. The LORD gave, and the LORD has taken away; Blessed be the name of the LORD." (Job 1:21 NKJV)

2. **Concerning the fulfillment of God's promises.**

"And not being weak in faith, he did not consider his own body, already dead (since he was about a hundred years old), and the deadness of Sarah's womb. (20) He did not waver at the promise of God through unbelief, but was strengthened in faith, giving glory to God, (21) and being fully convinced that what He had promised He was also able to perform. (22) And therefore, "it was accounted to him for righteousness." (Romans 4:19-22 NKJV)

Abraham patiently waited for God's promise.

3. **In respect of patient perseverance in well-doing.**

"For it is better, if it is the will of God, to suffer for doing good than for doing evil. (18) For Christ also suffered once for sins, the just for the unjust, that He might bring us to God, being put to death in the flesh but made alive by the Spirit." (1 Peter 3:17-18 NKJV)

4. **In bearing the infirmities of the brethren.**

"We then who are strong ought to bear with the scruples of the weak, and not to please ourselves. (2) Let each of us please his neighbor for his good, leading to edification. (3) For even Christ did not please Himself; but as it is written, "The reproaches of those who reproached You fell on Me." (Romans 15:1-3 NKJV)

Are you bearing with the weakness of others?

5. To bear, moreover, the unjust suspicion of others.

"Beloved, do not think it strange concerning the fiery trial which is to try you, as though some strange thing happened to you; (13) but rejoice to the extent that you partake of Christ's sufferings, that when His glory is revealed, you may also be glad with exceeding joy. (14) If you are reproached for the name of Christ, blessed are you, for the Spirit of glory and of God rests upon you. On their part He is blasphemed, but on your part He is glorified." (1 Peter 4:12-14 NKJV)

With joy - we suffer

6. To receive reproof.

"And you have forgotten the exhortation which speaks to you as to sons: "My son, do not despise the chastening of the LORD, Nor be discouraged when you are rebuked by Him; (6) For whom the LORD loves He chastens, And scourges every son whom He receives." (Hebrews 12:5-6 NKJV)

Patience with God's heavy hand.

Question 5: How are you displaying this kind of longsuffering? Are you quietly thankful to see God's hand working in your life – both good and bad?

The Spirit works the capacity of longsuffering, the power to bear without murmuring, to endure without complaint, and during times of grief.

Let me point out what longsuffering is NOT.

The "martyr complex" –

"Oh, I'm suffering for Jesus – look at me. You don't appreciate all I do for you. I will quietly endure, bearing my cross, even if you overlook my sufferings."

But if you have this martyr complex, you might look like you are longsuffering. Still, you express your bitterness by complaining, internally or to others, about others' lack of appreciation.

This type of "suffering" is NOT longsuffering – this is a sinful, self-focused spirit that wants others to pity them. And if they don't – you hold a grudge and bitterness in your heart.

Question 6: Ask yourself – am I merely playing the martyr, to get others to feel "my pain?" Are you holding a grudge of bitterness? The Lord has been longsuffering toward you – repent and ask for forgiveness.

Illustration: of Longsuffering from the Old Testament

Several examples from the Old Testament:

Joseph – quietly suffered a long time. We already looked at Joseph as a type of Christ. (Genesis 37-50)

Question 7: What do you remember of Joseph quietly suffering?

Isaiah's account of the Lord's "Suffering Servant" in Isaiah 52:13 – 53:12. We read and see how Jesus suffered and took upon Himself our sins.

Question 8: What do you remember about Isaiah's description of the Suffering Servant – Jesus?

Let's look at Job and his longsuffering.

Job – a model of Christ's patience and longsuffering

> "Therefore be patient, brethren, until the coming of the Lord. See how the farmer waits for the precious fruit of the earth, waiting patiently for it until it receives the early and latter rain. (8) You also be patient. Establish your hearts, for the coming of the Lord is at hand. (9) Do not grumble against one another, brethren, lest

you be condemned. Behold, the Judge is standing at the door! (10)
My brethren, take the prophets, who spoke in the name of the Lord,
as an example of suffering and patience. (11) Indeed we count
them blessed who endure. You have heard of the perseverance of
Job and seen the end intended by the Lord--that the Lord is very
compassionate and merciful." (James 5:7-11 NKJV)

Job: losses everything, falsely accused as to the reason for his loss by his friends, and in the end, restored. (A glimpse of the Gospel?)

Job asks many times, "Why have You forsaken me?" like Jesus asked from the Cross, "Why have You forsaken me?"

Let's do a brief overview of Job: Satan was permitted to destroy and kill

"Then Job arose, tore his robe, and shaved his head; and he fell to
the ground and worshiped. (21) And he said: "Naked I came from
my mother's womb, And naked shall I return there. The LORD
gave, and the LORD has taken away; Blessed be the name of
the LORD." (22) In all this, Job did not sin nor charge God with
wrong." (Job 1:20-22 NKJV)

"And he took for himself a potsherd with which to scrape himself
while he sat in the midst of the ashes. (9) Then his wife said to
him, "Do you still hold fast to your integrity? Curse God and die!"
(10) But he said to her, "You speak as one of the foolish women
speaks. Shall we indeed accept good from God, and shall we not
accept adversity?" In all this, Job did not sin with his lips." (Job
2:8-10 NKJV)

Yet in all the affliction from Satan and Job's friends – Job had one hope - **Job 19**– Job describes his suffering, which reflects the suffering of Christ. Yet, Job can say:

"For I know that my Redeemer lives, And He shall stand at last
on the earth." (Job 19:25 NKJV)

Job 42: Job suffered a significant loss - everything except his life. He lost his family; he lost his health; he lost his standing in the community. Yet in all this, Job remained faithful to the Lord.

God's judgment on the three friends:

> *"Do not grumble against one another, brethren, lest you be condemned. Behold, the Judge is standing at the door!" (James 5:9 NKJV)*

Job was restored, and Job interceded for his friends.

> *"Indeed we count them blessed who endure. You have heard of the perseverance of Job and seen the end intended by the Lord--that the Lord is very compassionate and merciful." (James 5:11 NKJV)*

Everything was restored; Job's wife gave birth to 10 more children.

Job is a story of a shadow type of the Gospel. Seeing his loss, his suffering, and being restored to greater glory.

Question 9: How do you see a glimpse of the Gospel in the life of Job?

Before we finish, let's return to the Cross

Application: Looking at Longsuffering from the Cross

"However, for this reason I obtained mercy, that in me first Jesus Christ might show all longsuffering, as a pattern to those who are going to believe on Him for everlasting life." (1 Timothy 1:16 NKJV)

"and consider that the longsuffering of our Lord is salvation--as also our beloved brother Paul, according to the wisdom given to him, has written to you," (2 Peter 3:15 NKJV)

During Jesus suffering – He said nothing to defend Himself. He could have called for help.

"Or do you think that I cannot now pray to My Father, and He will provide Me with more than twelve legions of angels?" (Matthew 26:53 NKJV)

In the time of our Savior, probably one legion would consist of 6,200-foot soldiers and 300 horses.

Twelve of which would amount to 74,400-foot soldiers, 3600 horses = 78,000 angels armed for battle. But Jesus chose to remain silent and endure the suffering ahead.

Question 10: Have you considered the silence of Jesus' suffering as His reaching out to you? Jesus chose to suffer at the hands of sinful men to bring salvation to all who would believe. How do you respond to Jesus' longsuffering?

Jesus had only one attitude toward those who were causing His suffering: **In silence, He suffered - praying: "Father forgive them; they do not know what they are doing."** (Luke 23:34) I can imagine Jesus having this attitude of forgiveness during the whole time of His passion; consider with me….

Imagine Jesus in His silence – praying…

Jesus is betrayed by Judas with a kiss and wrongfully arrested – **In silence.**

Jesus is abandoned by His disciples - **In silence.**

Jesus is falsely charged to be put to death – **In silence.**

Jesus is spat upon in His face, blindfolded Him, beaten, slapped by those of the Sanhedrin – "who hit you?" **In silence.**

Jesus is denied by Peter - **In silence.**

Jesus is bound and led to Pontius Pilate – **In silence.**

Jesus is retained over Barabbas – **In silence.**

Jesus is condemned by the crowd, "Crucify Him.!" – **In silence.**

Jesus is scourged and flogged at Pilate's command before sending Him to be crucified - **In silence.**

Jesus is humiliated by soldiers; scarlet robe, the crown of thorns – **In silence.**

Jesus is mocked; "Hail, King of the Jews." **In silence.**

Jesus is spat upon by the soldiers, mocking Him, hitting His head with a reed, pulling out His beard. **In silence.**

Jesus is forced to carry His Cross to Calvary – **In silence.**

Jesus is stripped of His clothing – **In silence.**

Jesus is crucified on a Cross – **Jesus does say: "Father forgive them."**

Jesus is mocked by the crowd wagging their heads – **In silence.**

Jesus is mocked by the religious leaders – "If You're the Christ, come down…"**In silence.**

Jesus is mocked by the two thieves – **In silence.**

Jesus is on the Cross for six hours, bearing our sins – At the very end, Jesus cries out in a loud voice: My God, My God, why have you forsaken me? Jesus' last words: "It is Finished" – He died.

Do you see Jesus' longsuffering for you? God has not destroyed you and taken you out – but waiting for you to repent – even you, Christian.

Are you still holding on to a grudge against another brother? Have you chosen to remain in your bitterness and withholding forgiveness?

Has God withheld forgiveness from you? No, He has not!

Question 11: How do you respond to these questions?

_____

_____

_____

_____

_____

Only one way to deal with your bitterness - Will you come daily to the Cross and let that blood cleans your heart?

> *"This, I recall to my mind; therefore, I have hope. (22) Through the LORD's mercies, we are not consumed, Because His compassions fail not. (23) They are new every morning; Great is Your faithfulness. (24) "The LORD is my portion," says my soul, "Therefore I hope in Him!" (Lamentations 3:21-24 NKJV)*

Will you come and be crucified with Christ and learn to walk in the Spirit?

Will you suffer in silence and pray, "Father, forgive them, forgive me for holding this grudge and not walking with You."

How often have you prayed, "The Lord's prayer?":

> *"And forgive us our debts, as we forgive our debtors." (Matthew 6:12 NKJV)*

If you have not forgiven – you are telling God – don't forgive me. Repent, ask God's forgiveness and ask forgiveness from those who you have hurt – seek reconciliation and leave it all at the foot of the Cross.

Kindness

*T*he context of the fruit of the Spirit in Galatians 5:22-23 is the battle going on within the Christian.

> *"I say then: Walk in the Spirit, and you shall not fulfill the lust of the flesh. (17) For the flesh lusts against the Spirit, and the Spirit against the flesh; and these are contrary to one another, so that you do not do the things that you wish. (18) But if you are led by the Spirit, you are not under the law." Galatians 5:16-18*

Paul gives a list of the works of the flesh (Galatians 5:19-20) then says, BUT….

> *"But the fruit of the Spirit is love, joy, peace, longsuffering, kindness, goodness, faithfulness, (23) gentleness, self-control. Against such there is no law." (Galatians 22-23 NKJV)*

And Paul brings the discussion back to the Gospel, back to the Cross:

> *"And those who are Christ's have crucified the flesh with its passions and desires. (25) If we live in the Spirit, let us also walk in the Spirit." (Galatians 5:24-25 NKJV)*

The only way to see the fruit of the Spirit in your life – is by coming to the Cross.

Remember: The Fruit is singular – with these "nine flavors" mixed. As we look at each "flavor" by itself – Do not forget the other eight.

Q: What is the flavor of Dr Pepper supposed to be?

A: Dr Pepper is a unique blend of 23 flavors. The formula for Dr Pepper is proprietary information. It tastes like carbonated prune juice to me. But I like prune juice.

Let's look at the Fifth quality of the Fruit of the Spirit: Kindness

So, in the last lesson we talked about longsuffering – the idea of silently suffering because of wickedness. Longsuffering is a PASSIVE response to sin toward us, to those who would do us harm. This word for kindness is the idea of ACTIVELY doing good to those who would harm us. So, in our "blend" of the fruit – in love, joy, and peace, we quietly suffer and show kindness to our enemies.

> *"Love suffers long and is kind; love does not envy; love does not parade itself, is not puffed up;" (1 Corinthians 13:4 NKJV)*

χρηστότης **chrēstótēs, khray-stot'-ace;** [G5544] from G5543; χρηστός chrēstós, khrase-tos' - the idea of usefulness, i.e., moral excellence (in character or demeanor):—gentleness, good(-ness), kindness.

This word is translated:

NKJV, NLT, NIV, ESV, RSV, NASB– kindness

KJV, WEB – gentleness (which expresses the character of kindness)

Practicing moral goodness, integrity, this kindness is gentle, mild, and pleasant. It is sweetness and kindness in a temper toward all, but toward ignorant and wicked in particular—the calmness of spirit, and unruffled disposition, treating all with politeness. Kindness is stooping to the lowest need, thinking nothing too small in which it may help, ready to give back a blessing for cursing, a benefit for harm and wrong. It is a useful kindness that benefits others with soothing to meet real needs in God's way. It is a service to others (always outward focused).

This is one of the expected effects of the Spirit's operations on the heart when we come to the Cross. It sweetens the temper, corrects an irritable disposition, makes the heart kind, disposes us to make all around us as happy as possible. This kindness is true politeness, kindhearted politeness, which can far better be learned in the school of Christ at the foot of the Cross.

As opposed to the works of the flesh: hatred, contentions, jealousies, outbursts of wrath, selfish ambitions, dissensions, envy, revelries, and the like, a harsh, crabbed, crooked temper, cruelty. Walking in the Spirit makes no one crabby, miserable, and sour.

Question 1: Can you say that kindness is a part of your character? Or are you the crabby, miserable, grumpy person? Are you walking in the Spirit or fulfilling the lusts of the flesh? Explain your answers.

_____

_____

_____

_____

_____

Let's look at kindness in God:

How does God demonstrate kindness toward us?

> *"Or do you despise the riches of His goodness (kindness) [G5544], forbearance, and longsuffering, not knowing that the goodness (kindness) [G5543] of God leads you to repentance?" (Romans 2:4 NKJV)*

Paul points us to the Cross - showing God's goodness/kindness leads us to repentance and to the Son. This is the message of the Gospel – it is the kindness of the Father that sent the Son to the Cross for us.

> *"Therefore, consider the goodness (kindness) [G5544], and severity of God: on those who fell, (speaking of the Jews who rejected the Gospel) severity; ……. but toward you (the Gentile believers), goodness (kindness) [G5544], if you continue in His goodness (kindness) [G5544]. Otherwise, you also will be cut off." (Romans 11:22 NKJV)*

(A warning of Paul concerning the "non-Christian" that thinks they are saved because they are in church.) Don't think that because God is kind – He is not severe to the wicked. If you have not repented and believed in the Son (i.e., rejecting Jesus as your Savior), then you only have God's wrath to look forward to.

> *"that in the ages to come He might show the exceeding riches of His grace in His kindness [G5544] toward us in Christ Jesus. (8) For by grace you have been saved through faith, and that not of yourselves; it is the gift of God, (9) not of works, lest anyone should boast. (10) For we are His workmanship, created in Christ Jesus for good works, which God prepared beforehand that we should walk in them." (Ephesians 2:7-10 NKJV)*

Paul points to the Gospel; God's kindness is seen in Christ Jesus; it is only by grace, are we saved through faith.

> *"For we ourselves were also once foolish, disobedient, deceived, serving various lusts and pleasures, living in malice and envy, hateful and hating one another. (4) BUT when the kindness [G5544] and the love of God our Savior toward man appeared, (5) not by works of righteousness which we have done, but according to His mercy He saved us, through the washing of regeneration and renewing of the Holy Spirit, (6) whom He poured out on us abundantly through Jesus Christ our Savior." (Titus 3:3-6 NKJV)*

Paul is again referencing the Gospel as our only hope and the way we ought to live – being washed by the blood, walking in the Spirit.

Question 2: Are you daily coming to the Cross to be washed? Are you coming to the Cross to find the power to walk in the Spirit? Are you coming to the Cross to war against your flesh that wants to do things contrary to the Lord? Have you, by faith, believed that Jesus personally died for you? Are you by faith walking in the Spirit? Explain your answers.

_____

_____

_____

_____

_____

So, how does kindness show itself in the believer?

How should believers demonstrate kindness toward others? *We start with the Cross.*

> *"I have been crucified with Christ; it is no longer I who live, but Christ lives in me; and the life which I now live in the flesh I live by faith in the Son of God, who loved me and gave Himself for me." (Galatians 2:20 NKJV)*

> *"And those who are Christ's have crucified the flesh with its passions and desires." (Galatians 5:24 NKJV)*

Believers ought to show "kindness:" kindness in action, kindness expressing itself in deeds. Kindness does not express itself in anger against sin, but in grace and tenderness and compassion."

Reminds me of Jesus with the woman at the well. In kindness, He confronted her concerning her sin and offered the solution. (John 4:1-42) With the woman caught in adultery, in kindness, Jesus confronted the Pharisees with their hypocrisy and told the women she was not condemned by Him – go and sin no more. (John 8:1-12)

Question 3: How would you describe and explain Jesus' dealing with sin in the above examples?

So, let's look at the believer and how to express kindness:

> *"They have all turned aside; They have together become unprofitable; There is none who does good (kindness) [G5544], no, not one." (Romans 3:12 NKJV) (Paul quoting Psalm 14:1, 3).*

We all are "naturally" without kindness. This kindness only comes from a changed heart that has been cut by the bloody Cross, and the Gospel is believed.

Paul describes the character of his ministry in 2 Corinthians and the means in how he endured all hardships:

> *"by purity, by knowledge, by longsuffering, by kindness [G5544], by the Holy Spirit, by sincere love, (7) by the word of truth, by the power of God, by the armor of righteousness on the right hand and on the left," (2 Corinthians 6:6-7 NKJV)*

Notice how many aspects of the fruit of Spirit are used in Paul's ministry. Within the context of the Gospel, Paul is protected with - "armor of righteousness." That righteousness is only applied as we come to the Cross and stand under the blood of righteousness that was poured out for us.

> *"Therefore, as the elect of God, holy and beloved, put on tender*
> *mercies, kindness [G5544], humility, meekness, longsuffering;"*
> *(Colossians 3:12 NKJV)*

Again, Paul "blends" these characteristics of the fruit of the Spirit and tells us to "put on" these qualities. And how do we "put on?" We yoke up with Jesus.

> *"Come to Me, all you who labor and are heavy laden, and I will*
> *give you rest. (29) "Take My yoke upon you and learn from Me,*
> *for I am gentle and lowly in heart, and you will find rest for your*
> *souls. (30) "For My yoke is easy and My burden is light." (Matthew*
> *11:28-30 NKJV)*

That word "easy" (from our root word χρηστός chrēstós, khrase-tos' G5543 - kind) When we are yoked up with Christ -we are walking with Him. Jesus' yoke is kind/gentle/easy on the neck.

> *"But if we walk in the light as He is in the light, we have fellowship*
> *with one another, and the blood of Jesus Christ His Son cleanses*
> *us from all sin." (1 John 1:7 NKJV)*

We walk with the blood of Jesus always in mind. There at the foot of the Cross, we see His blood cleansing us daily, moment by moment.

Question 4: Who are you yoked up with? Jesus? The world? Your flesh? It would not take long to determine which yoke you are wearing. Are you yoked up to the Cross of Christ, or are you yoked up to the bondage of sin? Explain your answers.

_____

_____

_____

_____

_____

Come and find the kindness of our Lord as you yoke up with Him at the Cross.

Let's turn our attention to the Old Testament and see an illustration of kindness and how it points us to the Gospel.

Illustration of Kindness from the Old Testament
David shows kindness to Mephibosheth **2 Samuel 4 / 2 Samuel 9**

David had made a covenant with Jonathan, his friend (**1 Samuel 18/20**)

> *"Then Jonathan said to David, "Go in peace, since we have both sworn in the name of the LORD, saying, 'May the LORD be between you and me, and between your descendants and my descendants, forever.' "So he arose and departed, and Jonathan went into the city." (1 Samuel 20:42 NKJV)*

David would see Jonathan one more time (1 Sam 23).

> *"And he said to him, "Do not fear, for the hand of Saul my father shall not find you. You shall be king over Israel, and I shall be next to you. Even my father Saul knows that." (18) So the two of them made a covenant before the LORD. And David stayed in the woods, and Jonathan went to his own house." (1 Samuel 23:17-18 NKJV)*

Both knew that David was destined for the throne to be king over Israel.

> *"Jonathan, Saul's son, had a son who was lame in his feet. He was five years old when the news about Saul and Jonathan came from Jezreel; (that they had been killed in battle) and his nurse took him up and fled. And it happened, as she made haste to flee, that he fell and became lame. His name was Mephibosheth." (2 Samuel 4:4 NKJV)*

Mephibosheth = "exterminating the idol" "Dispeller of shame."

He was the son of Jonathan and grandson of Saul.

David has been established, King over all of Israel, and all the battles have been fought. There is peace in the land. Now the kingdom is running smoothly – David remembers his friend Jonathan: I can imagine: Oh, if only my friend Jonathan were here with me know. Now David said:

> *"Is there still anyone who is left of the house of Saul, that I may show him kindness for Jonathan's sake?" (2 Samuel 9:1 NKJV)*

David was not aware of any of Saul's family and, particularly, from Jonathan's family survived. Then a servant from the house of Saul was called before David:

> *"Then the king said, "Is there not still someone of the house of Saul, to whom I may show the kindness of God?" And Ziba said to the king, "There is still a son of Jonathan who is lame in his feet." (2 Samuel 9:3 NKJV)*

David inquired and found where Mephibosheth was living. David sent for him, and Mephibosheth was brought out to come before David.

> *"Now when Mephibosheth, the son of Jonathan, the son of Saul, had come to David, he fell on his face and prostrated himself. Then David said, "Mephibosheth?" And he answered, "Here is your servant!" (2 Samuel 9:6 NKJV)*

David called him by name. Not clear if it was a question (Mephibosheth is that you?) or an exclamation (Mephibosheth – it's you!) But David recognized Mephibosheth – remember him as a child? Looks like his dad, Jonathan?

> *"So David said to him, "Do not fear, for I will surely show you kindness for Jonathan your father's sake, and will restore to you all the land of Saul your grandfather; and you shall eat bread at my table continually." (8) Then he bowed himself, and said, "What is your servant, that you should look upon such a dead dog as I?" (2 Samuel 9:7-8 NKJV)*

David remembered his covenant with Jonathan and cared for Mephibosheth. David charges Ziba, the servant – take care of all that I have given to Mephibosheth.

> *"Then Ziba said to the king, "According to all that my lord the king has commanded his servant, so will your servant do." "As for Mephibosheth," said the king, "he shall eat at my table like one of the king's sons." (2 Samuel 9:11 NKJV)*

> *"So Mephibosheth dwelt in Jerusalem, for he ate continually at the king's table. And he was lame in both his feet." (2 Samuel 9:13 NKJV)*

Question 5: Where do you see the Gospel in this story?

Let's connect the "Gospel dots" here in this historical narrative:

Remember, Mephibosheth was "lame" - that word for "lame" is the same word that is used in **Exodus 12** when the Lord will "pass over you" when the blood was applied to the doorpost during that first Passover.

The Lord "passed over" Mephibosheth (keeping him alive) that he might later be blessed by a covenant made between David and Jonathon.

> *"In that day," says the LORD, "I will assemble the lame, I will gather the outcast And those whom I have afflicted; (7) I will make the lame a remnant, And the outcast a strong nation; So the LORD will reign over them in Mount Zion From now on, even forever." (Micah 4:6-7 NKJV)*

God the Father made a covenant with God the Son to "pass over" the lame and gather them together as a remnant. Mephibosheth called himself a "dead dog." So, we are dead in our sins and trespasses. But the kindness of the Lord brought us to the table to feast with the King. There at the Cross, we find the Lord's kindness bringing us to Himself. (John 12:32)

The Lord restored all of Saul's land and property and assigned Ziba to care for him. The Lord has given us all the riches in glory (Philippians 4:19) and blessed us with every spiritual blessing in the heavenly places in Christ. (Ephesians 1:3) Like Ziba, to watch over Mephibosheth's well-being, we have been given the Holy Spirit to watch over us.

Question 6: How do you see the kindness of the Lord and the Gospel here in this story of David and Mephibosheth?

_____

_____

_____

_____

_____

_____

Application: Looking at Kindness from the Cross

This word for kindness is the idea of ACTIVELY doing good to those who would harm us. Jesus went to the Cross for us. Can you hear the kindness of the Lord calling you to come?

> *"Come near to Me, hear this: I have not spoken in secret from the beginning; From the time that it was, I was there. And now the Lord GOD and His Spirit Have sent Me." (Isaiah 48:16 NKJV)*

> *"Incline your ear, and come to Me. Hear, and your soul shall live; And I will make an everlasting covenant with you--The sure mercies of David." (Isaiah 55:3 NKJV)*

> *"Come to Me, all you who labor and are heavy laden, and I will give you rest." (Matthew 11:28 NKJV)*

Question 7: How have you come and found your rest here at the Cross?

> *"Now is the judgment of this world; now the ruler of this world will be cast out. (32) "And I, if I am lifted up from the earth, will draw all peoples to Myself." (33) This He said, signifying by what death He would die." (John 12:31-33 NKJV)*

> *"And as Moses lifted up the serpent in the wilderness, even so must the Son of Man be lifted up," (John 3:14 NKJV)*

"who Himself bore our sins in His own body on the tree, that we, having died to sins, might live for righteousness--by whose stripes you were healed." (1 Peter 2:24 NKJV)

Question 8: Do you see Jesus lifted up on the Cross, bearing your sins? Do you see Jesus bleeding out His life that you may have a life to the fullest? Explain your answers.

_____

_____

_____

_____

_____

_____

"I drew them with gentle cords, With bands of love, And I was to them as those who take the yoke from their neck. I stooped and fed them." (Hosea 11:4 NKJV)

"Come to Me, all you who labor and are heavy laden, and I will give you rest. (29) "Take My yoke upon you and learn from Me, for I am gentle and lowly in heart, and you will find rest for your souls. (30) "For My yoke is easy and My burden is light." (Matthew 11:28-30 NKJV)

Question 9: Are you yoked up to Jesus? Are you consciously walking daily coming to the Cross, finding your rest? Are you walking in the Spirit? Is the fruit of kindness evident in your life? Explain your answers.

"And they sang a new song, saying: "You are worthy to take the scroll, And to open its seals; For You were slain, And have redeemed us to God by Your blood Out of every tribe and tongue and people and nation," (Revelation 5:9 NKJV)

Goodness

The context of the fruit of the Spirit in Galatians 5:22-23 is the battle going on within the Christian.

> *"I say then: Walk in the Spirit, and you shall not fulfill the lust of the flesh. (17) For the flesh lusts against the Spirit, and the Spirit against the flesh; and these are contrary to one another, so that you do not do the things that you wish. (18) But if you are led by the Spirit, you are not under the law." Galatians 5:16-18*

Paul gives a list of the works of the flesh (Galatians 5:19-20) then says, BUT....

> *"But the fruit of the Spirit is love, joy, peace, longsuffering, kindness, goodness, faithfulness, (23) gentleness, self-control. Against such there is no law." (Galatians 5:22-23 NKJV)*

And Paul brings the discussion back to the Gospel, back to the Cross:

> *"And those who are Christ's have crucified the flesh with its passions and desires. (25) If we live in the Spirit, let us also walk in the Spirit." (Galatians 5:24-25 NKJV)*

The only way to see the fruit of the Spirit in your life – is by coming to the Cross.

As we go through these lessons, we will always be coming from the perspective of the Cross. There is no better filter than wearing our "Gospel glasses" and reading God's word with the Cross always in mind.

Let's look at the sixth quality of the Fruit of the Spirit: Goodness

Walking in the Spirit in Goodness

- How is the word "goodness" used in the Bible?
- We will look at an illustration from the Old Testament showing goodness.
- How does the Cross and the Gospel, Jesus' death, burial, and resurrection demonstrate goodness?

What is Goodness?

ἀγαθωσύνη **agathōsýnē,** [G19] goodness - agathos-synē; from root word [G18] (agathos); good: goodness, the idea of bigheartedness:—goodness. This particular word is only used four times in the New Testament.

Good (agathos)

Let's look at the root word good [G18] (agathos), so we can understand [G19] goodness - agathos-synē.

> *"Even so, every good **[G18] (agathos)**tree bears good **[G2570] (kalos)** fruit, but a bad tree bears bad fruit. (18) "A good **[G18] (agathos)** tree cannot bear bad fruit, nor can a bad tree bear good **[G2570] (kalos)** fruit." (Matthew 7:17-18 NKJV)*

The first good [G18] **(agathos)** is the idea of a good constitution, upright, honorable. We would say that a house has a good foundation.

The second good [G2570] (kalos) is the idea something is beautiful, excellent, precious. The idea of the fruit or the result that came out of what was good [G18] (agathos). This second good [G2570] (kalos) is the word used in the LXX (Greek Old Testament) in reference to God calling each day of creation as good [G2570] (kalos) and was very good [G2570] (kalos) at the end of the sixth day. (Genesis 1: 1-31) It was good because the creation came out of a God who was upright, honorable, and of good constitution.

Question 1: The Fruit of the Spirit can only come from a Good God working in your life. How does coming to the Cross build a "good" foundation to produce good fruit in your life?

How do we know God is good? Jesus said so:

> *"Now behold, one came and said to Him, "Good (agathos) Teacher, what good (agathos) thing shall I do that I may have eternal life?" (17) So He said to him, "Why do you call Me good (agathos)? No one is good (agathos) but One, that is, God. But if you want to enter into life, keep the commandments." (Matthew 19:16-17 NKJV)*

We see Jesus saying that there is only One who is good, and that is God Himself.

Question 2: How do you know, and why do you believe that God has been good in your life?

Consider another use of the word good (agathos).

> *"But one thing is needed, and Mary has chosen that good (agathos) part, which will not be taken away from her." (Luke 10:42 NKJV)*

Mary sat at Jesus' feet, drinking in all that Jesus was saying. Her focus was riveted on Jesus – she was not busy in the kitchen like Martha worried about fixing lunch. Mary had her priorities right. I like to think – what if both Mary and Martha were sitting at Jesus' feet? I think Jesus would have leaned over to the ladies and say, "Why don't we go into the kitchen and get lunch ready for the guys. We can continue our discussion." When we choose the good, the Lord will take care of those things that are important.

Question 3: What are you doing to "choose the good" when coming to the Cross?

_____

_____

_____

_____

_____

Paul uses this word good (agathos) as he reflects on his struggle with sin.

> *"For I know that in me (that is, in my flesh) nothing good (agathos) dwells; for to will is present with me, but how to perform what is good [G2570] (kalos) I do not find. (19) For the good (agathos) that I will to do, I do not do; but the evil I will not to do, that I practice." (Romans 7:18-19 NKJV)*

Paul is describing this battle between the Spirit and the flesh like in Galatians 5. And notice Paul's solution to this battle:

"O wretched man that I am! Who will deliver me from this body of death? (25) I thank God--through Jesus Christ our Lord! So then, with the mind I myself serve the law of God, but with the flesh the law of sin." (Romans 7:24-25 NKJV)

Keep reading ->

"There is therefore now no condemnation to those who are in Christ Jesus, who do not walk according to the flesh, but according to the Spirit. (2) For the law of the Spirit of life in Christ Jesus has made me free from the law of sin and death. (3) For what the law could not do in that it was weak through the flesh, God did by sending His own Son in the likeness of sinful flesh, on account of sin: He condemned sin in the flesh." (Romans 8:1-3 NKJV)

Paul brings us back to the Cross and to the Gospel of Jesus' death, burial, and resurrection as the only solution to sin in our lives. It is in the light of the Gospel; it is in the power of the Gospel we walk all the days of our lives.

Question 4: Can you identify with this spiritual battle? How does coming to the Cross assure you that ALL your sins have been dealt with once and for all?

Let's focus on this fruit of Goodness.
Goodness (agathos-syne)

  [G19] goodness - agathos-synē it means: uprightness of heart and life, goodness, kindness - a kindly activity toward those who don't deserve it. This goodness represents a rather more positive tendency of character in the sense of active compassion toward those who have sinned against us.

Isn't that what Paul teaches?

> "Therefore "If your enemy is hungry, feed him; If he is thirsty, give him a drink; For in so doing you will heap coals of fire on his head." (21) Do not be overcome by evil, but overcome evil with good. [G18] (agathos)" (Romans 12:20-21 NKJV)

Goodness is that character in us to hurt none, but to do ALL the good we can to all: A compassionate and charitable nature, with all that is kind, soft, winning, and tender, either in our mood or behavior,

If you are walking in the Spirit – this goodness will be seen.

Only from the Christian is this goodness seen. This word is only used 4 times in the Greek NT.

The focus of the fruit of goodness [G19] agathos-synē is looking at the core foundation within the believer of what is good that only comes from a personal, growing relationship with Jesus.

Let's briefly look at these 4 times the word agathos-synē is used.

> **1.** *"Now I myself am confident concerning you, my brethren, that you also are full of goodness* **[G19] agathos-synē**, *filled with all knowledge, able also to admonish one another."* (Romans 15:14 NKJV)

How do we admonish – that doesn't sound like goodness? Being full of goodness, we admonish in the spirit of Galatians 6:1:

> "Brethren, if a man is overtaken in any trespass, you who are spiritual restore such a one in a spirit of gentleness (an aspect of the fruit in a few weeks – remember they all blend), considering yourself lest you also be tempted." (Galatians 6:1 NKJV)

Question 5: How has the Lord given you a spirit of goodness when you correct and help someone who has fallen into sin?

In the next three verses, we find our word: [G19] agathos-synē

2. *"But the fruit of the Spirit is love, joy, peace, longsuffering, kindness, goodness [G19] agathos-synē, faithfulness," (Galatians 5:22 NKJV)*

Paul uses the word again when describing the fruit of the Spirit.

3. *"(for the fruit of the Spirit is in all goodness [G19] agathos-synē, righteousness, and truth)," (Ephesians 5:9 NKJV)*

Extra qualities of the fruit here (I won't add these). But quickly when you read the fruit of the Spirit is righteousness and truth – do you see that these qualities point us to Jesus and the Cross? Where does our righteousness come from?

"For He made Him who knew no sin to be sin for us, that we might become the righteousness of God in Him." (2 Corinthians 5:21)

Where do we go for truth?

"Jesus said to him, "I am the way, the truth, and the life. No one comes to the Father except through Me." (John 14:6 NKJV)

Only through the Cross are we able to come before God as righteous because we went through the Truth, Jesus. We do not muster-up these fruits in our own strength and self-will. It is Holy Spirit produced.

And the last verse:

> 4. *"Therefore, we also pray always for you that our God would count you worthy of this calling, and fulfill all the good pleasure of His goodness [G19] agathos-synē and the work of faith with power, (12) that the name of our Lord Jesus Christ may be glorified in you, and you in Him, according to the grace of our God and the Lord Jesus Christ."* *(2 Thessalonians 1:11-12 NKJV)*

Paul's prayer for the church, in light of the Gospel, God's goodness would fill us… - our faith would be seen with power, and the name of Jesus would be glorified. Oh, may this be the testimony of His church around the world and this church as the fruit of the Spirit matures and grows in each one of us.

Question 6: How are you growing in goodness?

Illustration: From the Old Testament – Hosea and Gomer and the goodness extended

Hosea and Gomer **Hosea 1 – 3**

Hosea 1 Hosea was asked to do something unbelievable – marry an actively practicing prostitute.

Why? – to illustrate how Israel had departed from the Lord and committed great harlotry. And it appears that the woman Hosea will marry, Gomer will continue to have children by other men while married to Hosea.

> *"When the LORD began to speak by Hosea, the LORD said to Hosea: "Go, take yourself a wife of harlotry And children of harlotry, For the land has committed great harlotry By departing from the LORD." (Hosea 1:2 NKJV)*

Hosea married Gomer:
Three children were born in the judgment of God toward Israel.

1. Jezreel: God will sow or that which God planted (Hosea 1:4)
The valley where Ahab's wife Jezebel (1 Kings 21:1-10); had Naboth killed for his vineyard. and Jehu killed Jezebel for her wickedness by the command of the Lord. (2 Kings 9:15)

2. Lo-Ruhamah: no mercy – (Hosea 1:6-7)
The Lord would cut off Israel and no longer show mercy

3. Lo-Ammi: not my people – (Hosea 1:8-9)
The Lord would now call Israel, "Not My people."
But there is a promise of hope: vs 10-11

> *"Yet the number of the children of Israel Shall be as the sand of the sea, Which cannot be measured or numbered. And it shall come to pass In the place where it was said to them, 'You are not My people,' There it shall be said to them, 'You are sons of the living God.' (11) Then the children of Judah and the children of Israel Shall be gathered together, And appoint for themselves one head (reference to Jesus); And they shall come up out of the land, For great will be the day of Jezreel!" (Hosea 1:10-11 NKJV)*

Question 7: How are you beginning to see Jesus in this first chapter of Hosea?

HOSEA 2 IS A CHAPTER OF THE LORD'S LOVE FOR HIS UNFAITHFUL PEOPLE.

The Lord will bring terrible things upon His people because Israel worshiped the Baals and forgot the Lord. The Lord has done the same with us at times. We find that our sins have left us miserable because we would rather do things "MY WAY" rather than follow the Lord. We have experienced the "No mercy" and being "Not my people." But the Lord would call us back by His mercy, those who are now My people.

Question 8: Describe how you have found yourself miserable because of some besetting sin in your life?

HOSEA 3 SHOWS US HOSEA'S LIFE AND GOODNESS TO HIS WIFE, GOMER.

A shadow of the Cross.

> *"Then the LORD said to me, "Go again, love a woman who is loved by a lover and is committing adultery, just like the love of the LORD for the children of Israel, who look to other gods and love the raisin cakes of the pagans." (Hosea 3:1 NKJV)*

Oh my! Now the Lord is telling Hosea to go back to this adulteress wife who has found herself sold into the slavery of prostitution.

Then Hosea obeys with an attitude of "not my will, but Yours be done."

> *"So I bought her for myself for fifteen shekels of silver, and one and one-half homers of barley." (Hosea 3:2 NKJV)*

Do you see Jesus? Jesus said that He would buy us from the slave market of sin. But it was the price of His blood, shed on the Cross. That blood has redeemed us.

Then Hosea says to Gomer:

> *"And I said to her, "You shall stay with me many days; you shall not play the harlot, nor shall you have a man--so, too, will I be toward you." (Hosea 3:3 NKJV)*

When Jesus redeems us, purchases us with His blood, we are now His; we are to stay with Him for many days (can you say forever?). We are to no longer practice the works of the flesh but walk in the Spirit because, like Hosea's goodness toward Gomer in purchasing her from slavery, Jesus has shown us His goodness at the Cross by purchasing us from our bondage of sin by His blood.

Question 9: How are you free from your bondages of sin? Have you come to the Cross, (even as a Christian) to find the blood of the Cross will free you from the slavery of sin?

"Now the works of the flesh are evident, which are: adultery, fornication, uncleanness, lewdness, (20) idolatry, sorcery, hatred, contentions, jealousies, outbursts of wrath, selfish ambitions, dissensions, heresies, (21) envy, murders, drunkenness, revelries, and the like; of which I tell you beforehand, just as I also told you in time past, that those who practice such things will not inherit the kingdom of God." (Galatians 5:19-21 NKJV)

Question 10: How are you beginning to find freedom from the bondage of sin at the Cross?

Application from the Cross

> *"when He (Jesus) comes, in that Day, to be glorified in His saints and to be admired among all those who believe, because our testimony among you was believed. (11) Therefore we also pray always for you that our God would count you worthy of this calling, and fulfill all the good pleasure of His goodness and the work of faith with power, (12) that the name of our Lord Jesus Christ may be glorified in you, and you in Him, according to the grace of our God and the Lord Jesus Christ."* (2 Thessalonians 1:10-12 NKJV)

I know the Pastor; the elders and others have been praying for you all that "God would count you worthy of this calling and fulfill all the good pleasure of His goodness and work of faith with power in your lives."

When we come to the Cross – we see Jesus' goodness, the uprightness of heart and life, goodness, kindness - a kindly activity on (the sinner's) behalf. Jesus has shown this goodness toward us sinners. There at the Cross, we see His love, joy, peace, longsuffering, kindness, gentleness, goodness, faithfulness, and self-control being directed toward us.

Question 11: In what areas do you find yourself on the slave block of sin? Are there those besetting sins that so easily ensnare you? Yes, even as a Christian, we can become in bondage to sin. Like Gomer, even after being married to Hosea, she could not leave her prostitution and found herself as a slave

We have only one hope – come back to the Cross and find that you have been purchased, you have been washed, the blood of the Lamb has redeemed you. Don't leave the Cross and find yourself worshipping some false god of pleasure, some false god of self-advancement, some false god of self-pride, self-accomplishments, self-whatever. As you come to the Cross – stay there and learn to sit at Jesus' feet and abide in Him. Make Jesus your first thought at the beginning of the day and your last thoughts as you go to bed – and everywhere in between. We call this walking is the Spirt.

The context of the fruit of the Spirit is a crucified life:

> *"I have been crucified with Christ; it is no longer I who live, but Christ lives in me; and the life which I now live in the flesh I live by faith in the Son of God, who loved me and gave Himself for me. (21) "I do not set aside the grace of God; for if righteousness comes through the law, then Christ died in vain." (Galatians 2:20-21 NKJV)*

> *"And those who are Christ's have crucified the flesh with its passions and desires. (25) If we live in the Spirit, let us also walk in the Spirit. (26) Let us not become conceited, provoking one another, envying one another." (Galatians 5:24-26 NKJV)*

Question 12: Are you learning to crucify the flesh with its passions and desires? Or are you still in bondage in practicing the works of the flesh? Explain your answers.

"Now the works of the flesh are evident, which are: adultery, fornication, uncleanness, lewdness, (20) idolatry, sorcery, hatred, contentions, jealousies, outbursts of wrath, selfish ambitions, dissensions, heresies, (21) envy, murders, drunkenness, revelries, and the like; of which I tell you beforehand, just as I also told you in time past, that those who practice such things will not inherit the kingdom of God." (Galatians 5:19-21 NKJV)

Jesus went to the Cross out of His goodness to purchase and redeem you. You don't need to be enslaved to selfish sins and desires. You are not under Law – There is no law against the fruit of the Spirit. Come to the Cross to be purchased from your slavery to sin. It has already been paid for in full. Come and be washed. Come to the Cross and learn how to walk in the Spirit. You will see this fruit in your lives as you walk in the Spirit. As you come to the Cross, washed clean by the blood, walking in the Spirit – you will be equipped to war against your flesh and find real victory by the power of the Gospel working in and through your life.

Faithfulness

A reminder: The context of the fruit of the Spirit in Galatians 5:22-23 is the battle going on **within the Christian**. The non-Christian does not have this type of conflict going on within.

> *"I say then: Walk in the Spirit, and you shall not fulfill the lust of the flesh. (17) For the flesh lusts against the Spirit, and the Spirit against the flesh; and these are contrary to one another, so that you do not do the things that you wish. (18) But if you are led by the Spirit, you are not under the law. ... (22) But the fruit of the Spirit is love, joy, peace, longsuffering, kindness, goodness, faithfulness, (23) gentleness, self-control. Against such there is no law." (Galatians 5:16-18, 22-23 NKJV):*

Remember walking in the Spirit – being fruitful starts and finishes with the Gospel, back to the Cross:

> *"And those who are Christ's have crucified the flesh with its passions and desires. (25) If we live in the Spirit, let us also walk in the Spirit." (Galatians 5:24-25 NKJV)*

Let's look at the seventh quality of the Fruit of the Spirit: Faithfulness.
We are going to look at three things in this lesson:

- How does the Bible define and use faithfulness?
- What illustration from the Old Testament shows faithfulness?
- How does the Cross demonstrate faithfulness?

What does faithfulness mean?

Preparing for this lesson has been an exciting word study for me. The word is πίστις pístis, [G4102], which is translated most of the time as **faith** in the New Testament. It comes from the root word from πείθω peíthō G3982; meaning to persuade, to be induced to believe.

This word faithfulness is the word for faith πίστις pístis. In its *biblical* sense, faith is always *received* by believers only (never self-generated). Faith is always the gift (work) of God, from the moment of the regeneration of our hearts and conversion to the end of our sanctification, and we see Jesus face to face.

Consider these verses from Ezekiel. Listen how many times God says: "I will…"

> *"Then I will sprinkle clean water on you, and you shall be clean; I will cleanse you from all your filthiness and from all your idols. (26) "I will give you a new heart and put a new spirit within you; I will take the heart of stone out of your flesh and give you a heart of flesh. (27) "I will put My Spirit within you and cause you to walk in My statutes, and you will keep My judgments and do them." Ezekiel 36:25-27 NKJV*

Ezekiel is pointing us to the Gospel, Jesus' death, burial, and resurrection:

- Only there at the Cross are we made clean from ALL our filthiness.
- Only at the Cross are we given a new heart and receive the Holy Spirit of promise.
- Only at the Cross do we find the power to walk in obedience because of the resurrection.

And it is God who said, "I will…" do these things in the heart of His people.

Question 1: Do you see how it is God who will work in you? Can you share when you first came to faith in Jesus Christ?

_____

_____

_____

_____

_____

_____

So, where does this faith come from?

> *"So, then faith comes by hearing, and hearing by the word of God."* **(Romans 10:17 NKJV)**

Faith comes by hearing - When we hear the Word (rhema) of God. Rhema means that which is or has been uttered by the living voice.
Jesus used this word rhema:

> *"But He answered and said, "It is written, 'Man shall not live by bread alone, but by every word* **(rhema)** *that proceeds from the mouth of God.' "* (*Matthew 4:4 NKJV*)

> *"All Scripture is given by inspiration of God, [God breathed] and is profitable for doctrine, for reproof, for correction, for instruction in righteousness, (17) that the man of God may be complete, thoroughly equipped for every good work."* (*2 Timothy 3:16-17 NKJV*)

Question 2: Are you hearing God's Word? How have you seen God speaking to you through the Bible?

_____

_____

_____

_____

_____

Paul used this word **hearing** in the context of faith in Galatians:

> *"This only I want to learn from you: Did you receive the Spirit by the works of the law, or by the **hearing of faith**? ... (5) Therefore He who supplies the Spirit to you and works miracles among you, does He do it by the works of the law, or by the **hearing of faith**?"* (*Galatians 3:2, 5 NKJV*)

So, how do we get this faith?

> *But God, who is rich in mercy, because of His great love with which He loved us, (5) "even when we were dead in trespasses, made us alive together with Christ (by grace you have been saved), (6) and raised us up together, and made us sit together in the heavenly places in Christ Jesus, (7) that in the ages to come He might show the exceeding riches of His grace in His kindness toward us in Christ Jesus. (8) For by grace, you have been saved through faith, and that not of yourselves; it is the gift of God, (9) not of works, lest anyone should boast. (10) For we are His workmanship, created in Christ Jesus for good works, which God prepared beforehand that we should walk in them." (Ephesians 2:4-10 NKJV)*

Faith is the gift of God, a gift of divine persuasion in what we believe.

Question 3: How do you know that you have received this gift of faith?

_____

_____

_____

_____

_____

Let's look at some other verses that use the word faith (pistis). Notice how faith is used to help us understand its use as faithfulness:

> *"Now faith is the substance (confidence, foundation, assurance, the reality), of things hoped for, the evidence of things not seen. (2) For by it (faith) the elders obtained a good testimony. (3) By faith we understand that the worlds were framed by the word of God, so that the things which are seen were not made of things which are visible." (Hebrews 11:1-3 NKJV)*

Faith pístis (G4102) is the conviction of the truth of everything we read in the Bible. There is a belief in the Bible, confidence or belief respecting man's relationship to God and divine things through the Cross's finished work. By faith, we overcome the world:

> *"For whatever is born of God overcomes the world. And this is the victory that has overcome the world--our faith. (5) Who is he who overcomes the world, but he who believes that Jesus is the Son of God?" (1 John 5:4-5 NKJV)*

Question 4: Fill in the blanks: "For whatever is born of God _____ the world. And this is the victory that has _____ the world-- _____ _____. (5) Who is he who _____ the world, but he who believes that Jesus is the Son of God?" (1 John 5:4-5 NKJV)

Faith **IS** all about Him, our triune God; our faith comes from Him and glorifies Him.

Faith then **IS NOT** the *same as human belief.* Faith is always God's work and gift into the believer:

> *"For I say, through the grace given to me, to everyone who is among you, not to think of himself more highly than he ought to think, but to think soberly, as God has dealt to each one a measure of faith." (Romans 12:3 NKJV)*

And how much faith do we need? – according to Jesus: the size of a mustard seed. (Matthew 17:20; Luke 17:6) Because it is the object of our faith that has the power – God Himself seen in the power of the Gospel. Faith is not in faith, not in yourself. "I have faith I can do this…" This is not "self-talk" or the power of positive thinking.

There is a lot of confusion about this "self-faith" that leads some to mistake faith as their "weapon" to wield supernatural power . . . [*for self-serving ends.*] (Can you say: "Name it and claim it?")

Listen to what Paul says:

> *"Therefore we also pray always for you that our God would count you worthy of this calling, and fulfill all the good pleasure of His goodness and the work of faith with power, (12) that the name of our Lord Jesus Christ may be glorified in you, and you in Him, according to the grace of our God and the Lord Jesus Christ." (2 Thessalonians 1:11-12 NKJV)*

Faith is a gift from God that is used for God's glory with power.

Faith is related to (yet distinct from believing (4100/pisteúō). Faith (a Greek noun) refers to "God's persuasion birthed in the believer." Believing (a

Greek verb) relates to the human choice to have confidence (affirm, trust) in what God says.

Faith is not exactly the same as *believing*, and *believing* is not exactly the same as *faith*.

["Faith is from God" *is distinct* from human *belief* and *confidence*, though they overlap in meaning.]

Demons believe (and shudder) ... but they do not have (experience) faith! And the demons are destined to hell.

> *"You believe that there is one God. You do well. Even the demons believe--and tremble!"* (*James 2:19 NKJV*)

My Testimony:

I always believed that there was a God – out there, somewhere. I just didn't know how to get there. I grew up going to church: heard Bible stories, on the same level as Grimm's fairytales. But then the Lord, at the age of twenty, in His providence, brought me to a family that believed and had faith in God. (I was to tutor of a ten-year-old in math to get three college credits.) They were showing faithfulness to their God. After three months of tutoring and getting to know this family – I went to their church two weeks before entering the Navy. There I heard the Gospel for the first time (Jesus died on a Cross for my sins, was buried, and rose from the grave on the third day) – the Lord replaced that heart of stone with a heart of flesh, and I believed that Jesus died for my sins and wanted to be in my life. That morning – I prayed, "God, I quit – come in and take over."

Faith (4102/*pístis*) is always *received from God* (*never* generated by people). Faith is always a response to a divine revelation.

"Faith . . . both in its initiation and every step of the way, is Spirit given . . . faith is *God-given*" We walk by faith and not by sight.

Question 5: How are you walking by faith daily?

_____

_____

_____

_____

_____

Believers should *keep growing* in God's gift of *faith "from faith into faith."* (Romans 1:17) This growth is likewise described as believers being transformed *"from glory to glory,"* as we behold the glory of the Lord. (2 Corinthians 3:18) This faith in the Gospel is coming to the Cross as we grow from faith to faith in our sanctification. It is this faithfulness of believing day by day we grow in the grace and knowledge of our Lord.

Reflection:

Many people *believe . . . without* having faith (like the demons) – and many have faith . . . but lack enough belief to carry it through! *"Lord I believe, help my unbelief."*

The Christian's life goal is only to do works of genuine faith, i.e., only what is inspired by God revealed from His Word. How do we know what "works" to do? We listen, read, study, memorize, meditate, and sing God's word. We make God's words our thoughts, and we, by faith - trust, and obey. There is no other way.

[Faith from God inspires (produces) *faith*-believing, i.e., faithfulness.

"For we walk by faith, not by sight." (*2 Corinthians 5:7 NKJV*)

Question 6: How is your time in God's word? What things are you doing on a daily basis to keep God's word in all of your thinking?

As we walk by faith – we become faithful in all we think, say, and do. Our walk with Jesus, walking in the Spirit, will become evident. By faith, we will walk away from the "works of the flesh: (Galatians 5:19-21) (also see Matthew 15:18-19)

Let's apply faith to the works of the flesh:

- by faith, we will not - commit adultery; instead, we go to the Cross
- by faith, we will not - commit fornication; instead, we go to the Cross
- by faith, we will not - display uncleanness; instead, we go to the Cross
- by faith, we will not - display lewdness; instead, we go to the Cross
- by faith, we will not - commit idolatry; instead, we go to the Cross
- by faith, we will not - commit sorcery; instead, we go to the Cross
- by faith, we will not - display hatred; instead, we go to the Cross
- by faith, we will not - display contentions; instead, we go to the Cross
- by faith, we will not - display jealousies; instead, we go to the Cross
- by faith, we will not - display outbursts of wrath; instead, we go to the Cross
- by faith, we will not - display selfish ambitions; instead, we go to the Cross
- by faith, we will not - display dissensions; instead, we go to the Cross
- by faith, we will not – be teaching heresies; instead, we go to the Cross
- by faith, we will not – display envy; instead, we go to the Cross
- by faith, we will not - commit murders; instead, we go to the Cross

- by faith, we will not - commit drunkenness; instead, we go to the Cross
- by faith, we will not - display revelries; instead, we go to the Cross
- by faith, we will not - display or commit "the like"; instead, we go to the Cross

- by faith we go to the Cross and have our flesh crucified with its passions and desires
- by faith we will walk in the Spirit
This is the fruit of faithfulness.

It is by faith – we walk away from our sinful fleshly desires and walk in the Spirit. How? We come by faith to the Cross to be washed in the blood (1 John 1:7), we continue by faith to walk in the Spirit with the Cross always in view (Galatians 2:20, 5:24), and by faith, we war against our sinful flesh, by applying and working out the fruit of the Spirit in our lives. As we walk in faith – we will be showing the quality of faithfulness in our lives. (Galatians 5:16-18)

Question 7: How are you going to the Cross to find the power to say, "No!" to the flesh and walk in the Spirit by faith?

Illustration: the faithfulness of Abraham
Paul uses an Old Testament illustration of faith:

"Therefore He who supplies the Spirit to you and works miracles among you, does He do it by the works of the law, or by the hearing of faith?-- (6) just as Abraham "believed God, and it

was accounted to him for righteousness." (7) Therefore know that only those who are of faith are sons of Abraham. (8) And the Scripture, foreseeing that God would justify the Gentiles by faith, preached the Gospel to Abraham beforehand, saying, "In you, all the nations shall be blessed." (9) So then those who are of faith are blessed with believing Abraham." (Galatians 3:5-9 NKJV)

What? Did God preach the Gospel to Abraham? Did God preach Jesus' death, burial, and resurrection to Abraham?

Paul was quoting in verse 8, a verse from **Genesis 22**:

"In your seed, all the nations of the earth shall be blessed because you have obeyed My voice." (Genesis 22:18 NKJV)

Let's read and consider how God preached the Gospel to Abraham in – **Genesis 22**

"Now it came to pass after these things that God tested Abraham, and said to him, "Abraham!" And he said, "Here I am." (2) Then He said, "Take now your son, your only son Isaac, whom you love, and go to the land of Moriah, and offer him there as a burnt offering on one of the mountains of which I shall tell you." (3) So Abraham rose early in the morning and saddled his donkey, and took two of his young men with him, and Isaac his son; and he split the wood for the burnt offering, and arose and went to the place of which God had told him." (Genesis 22:1-3 NKJV)

Here is a hard request from God – yet Abraham immediately obeyed and left with his son, Isaac, wood for the offering, with two young men early the next morning.

"Then, on the third day, Abraham lifted his eyes and saw the place afar off. (5) And Abraham said to his young men, "Stay here with the donkey; the lad and I will go yonder and worship, and we will come back to you." (Genesis 22:4-5 NKJV)

On the third day – Abraham arrived at the appointed place. Told the two young men to stay, and he and Isaac will return after worshipping.

> "So Abraham took the wood of the burnt offering and laid it on Isaac, his son; and he took the fire in his hand, and a knife and the two of them went together. (7) But Isaac spoke to Abraham, his father, and said, "My father!" And he said, "Here I am, my son." Then he said, "Look, the fire, and the wood, but where is the lamb for a burnt offering?" (8) And Abraham said, "My son, God will provide for Himself the lamb for a burnt offering." So the two of them went together." (Genesis 22:6-8 NKJV)

The wood is placed upon Isaac to carry up the hill. Abraham takes the fire and knife for the sacrifice. Isaac asked a simple question: "Where is the lamb for the burnt offering?" Good question: answer – God will provide for Himself a lamb.

> "Then they came to the place of which God had told him. And Abraham built an altar there and placed the wood in order; and he bound Isaac his son and laid him on the altar, upon the wood. (10) And Abraham stretched out his hand and took the knife to slay his son. (11) But the Angel of the LORD called to him from heaven and said, "Abraham, Abraham!" So he said, "Here I am." (12) And He said, "Do not lay your hand on the lad, or do anything to him; for now I know that you fear God, since you have not withheld your son, your only son, from Me." (13) Then Abraham lifted his eyes and looked, and there behind him was a ram caught in a thicket by its horns. So, Abraham went and took the ram, and offered it up for a burnt offering instead of his son. (14) And Abraham called the name of the place, The-LORD-Will-Provide; as it is said to this day, "In the Mount of the LORD it shall be provided." (Genesis 22:9-14 NKJV)

There on this specific spot – Abraham was ready to sacrifice his only son – God stopped him and provided a ram for the sacrifice.

"Then the Angel of the LORD called to Abraham a second time out of heaven, (16) and said: "By Myself, I have sworn, says the LORD, because you have done this thing, and have not withheld your son, your only son-- (17) "blessing I will bless you, and multiplying I will multiply your descendants as the stars of the heaven and as the sand which is on the seashore; and your descendants shall possess the gate of their enemies. (18) "In your seed, all the nations of the earth shall be blessed, because you have obeyed My voice." (19) So Abraham returned to his young men, and they rose and went together to Beersheba; and Abraham dwelt at Beersheba." (Genesis 22:15-19 NKJV)

Question 8: What details of the Gospel did you see in Genesis 22?

Let me go back and point out how God preached the Gospel to Abraham.

- Take your only son (vs. 2) – Like God, the Father took His only Son to be a sacrifice.
- To the land of Moriah (vs. 2) – the place where Jerusalem would be built. Later, the temple was built; all the sacrifices of the Lord were there in Jerusalem. So, Jesus would be sacrificed on the Cross there in Jerusalem.
- It was on the third day that Isaac was spared. (vs. 4) For three days, Isaac was as good as dead as they traveled to the place appointed by God. So, Jesus was dead for three days.

- Isaac carried the wood on his back up the hill. (vs. 6) Like Jesus, who carried the wooden Cross up the hill of Calvary.
- Isaac asked, where is the Lamb? (vs. 7) God would provide His perfect lamb: Behold the Lamb of God who takes away the sin of the world.
- Isaac was bound and placed upon the wood. And there is no record of any struggle from Isaac – he yielded to his father's will. (vs. 9) Jesus yielded to the Father's will – "Not My will, but Yours be done." Jesus was bound to the Cross by three nails of the crucifixion. (I do not know for sure where Abraham built the alter – some say at Calvary, the very spot where Jesus would die, others say on the sight of the temple. Either way – Jesus' became the bloody sacrifice for us.)
- God stopped Abraham (vs. 11-12) but concerning Jesus – the Father did not stop, and the judgment and wrath of the Father toward sin was poured out upon His Son. God's knife of wrath plunged deep into the heart of Jesus.
- And at the end of that third day for Abraham and Isaac – Isaac was resurrected. *"By faith Abraham, when he was tested, offered up Isaac, and he who had received the promises offered up his only begotten son, (18) of whom it was said, "In Isaac your seed shall be called," (19) concluding that God was able to raise him up, even from the dead, from which he also received him in a figurative sense."* **(Hebrews 11:17-19 NKJV)**

Like Jesus, who died and rose on the third day.

- The promise that "the Seed will bless all" is expounded upon by Paul:

  "Now to Abraham and his Seed were the promises made. He does not say, "And to seeds," as of many, but as of one, "And to your Seed," who is Christ. (17) And this I say, that the law, which was four hundred and thirty years later, cannot annul the covenant that was confirmed before by God in Christ, that it should make the promise of no effect. (18) For if the inheritance is of the law, it is no longer of promise; but God gave it to Abraham by promise." (Galatians 3:16-18 NKJV)

The Gospel was clearly preached to Abraham there on that mount of sacrifice. Let's turn our attention once more to the Cross.

Question 9: Fill in the blank: "And the Scripture, foreseeing that God would _____ the Gentiles by _____, _____ the _____ to Abraham beforehand, saying, "In you, all the nations shall be blessed." (Galatians 3:8 NKJV)

Application: Let's look at the faithfulness of Jesus at the Cross

Hebrews 12:1-3 – Jesus by faith – went to the Cross for us. Jesus was faithful to His calling.

> *"Therefore we also, since we are surrounded by so great a cloud of witnesses, let us lay aside every weight, and the sin which so easily ensnares us, and let us run with endurance the race that is set before us, (2) looking unto Jesus, the **author** [chief leader, one that takes the lead and becomes an example, a trail blazer] and **finisher** [perfector, one who set before us the highest example] of our faith, who for the joy that was set before Him endured the Cross, despising the shame, and has sat down at the right hand of the throne of God. (3) For consider Him who endured such hostility from sinners against Himself, lest you become weary and discouraged in your souls." (Hebrews 12:1-3 NKJV)*

Jesus had faith that the Father would raise Him up on the third day:

> *"Therefore, my heart is glad, and my glory rejoices; My flesh also will rest in hope. (10) For You will not leave my soul in Sheol, Nor will You allow Your Holy One to see corruption. (11) You will show me the path of life; In Your presence is fullness of joy; At Your right hand are pleasures forevermore." (Psalm 16:9-11 NKJV)*

Question 10: How have you had this experience, receiving this heart of gladness and joy? It is the Lord who gives us this heart that we hear the Gospel.

_____

_____

_____

_____

_____

> *"So then faith comes by hearing, and hearing by the word of God."*
> (*Romans 10:17 NKJV*)

> *"For I am not ashamed of the Gospel of Christ, for it is the power of God to salvation for everyone who believes, for the Jew first and also for the Greek. (17) For in it, the righteousness of God is revealed from faith to faith; as it is written, "The just shall live by faith." (Romans 1:16-17 NKJV)*

Are you living by faith?
Listen to Jesus' words:

> *"Jesus said to him, "I am the way, the truth, and the life. No one comes to the Father except through Me." (John 14:6 NKJV)*

Is Jesus outside of the church for you?

> *"Behold, I stand at the door and knock. If anyone hears My voice and opens the door, I will come into him and dine with him, and he with Me." (Revelation 3:20 NKJV)*

The "Call to worship:" made by the Pastor (who is representing us before God) is **<u>NOT</u>** calling to God –

"Okay – come in here; we are ready now."

We think Jesus is at the door of the church asking–

"Can I come in now?"

No! – The "Call to worship:" made by the Pastor (who is representing and the spokesmen for God) is God calling us to come into His presence to worship Him. The triune God is already here – He is inviting you to come and worship.

Question 11: Do you go to church by faith and worship every week? How is your faithfulness evident to all? How do you share the hope of the Cross to those at church?

By God's grace, we find ourselves faithful as we come to worship and be pointed to the Cross. We are reminded to die to self and walk with the Spirit.

Can you say, "Yes, I believe and have faith in the finished work of Jesus on the Cross, and by faith, I am walking with Him by God's grace, I am faithful."?

Gentleness

*T*he context of the fruit of the Spirit in Galatians 5:22-23 is the battle going on within the Christian. The Galatian church listened to another gospel based upon the "working the program" of law-keeping.

Paul starts at the beginning of chapter five concerning being entangled again with a yoke of bondage: bondage to the Law to make oneself more righteous. Working the program of law-keeping (self-effort) to obtain righteousness apart from the Cross. Paul has only had one message in his ministry:

> *"For I determined not to know anything among you except Jesus Christ and Him crucified." (1 Corinthians 2:2 NKJV)*

Notice how Paul begins this epistle:

> *"Paul, an apostle (not from men nor through man, but through Jesus Christ and God the Father who raised Him from the dead)"* (*Galatians 1:1 NKJV*)

The Gospel, Jesus' death, burial, and resurrection, is always in his thinking as he writes to the church. The Gospel is the foundation of Paul's thought. And you will find some references to the Gospel with keywords in every chapter. You can read these later.

Gospel- Galatians 1:6-9,11; 2:5-7,14; 3:8; 4:4-6; 4:13
Cross- Galatians 5:11, 6:12,14
Crucified- Galatians 2:20-21; 3:1; 5:24; 6:14

Paul brings the church to where the real power lies to walk in freedom from sin. He brings them to the Cross. Here we find the power in the Gospel to walk in the Spirit.

"I say then: Walk in the Spirit, and you shall not fulfill the lust of the flesh. (17) For the flesh lusts against the Spirit, and the Spirit against the flesh; and these are contrary to one another, so that you do not do the things that you wish. (18) But if you are led by the Spirit, you are not under the law..... (22) But the fruit of the Spirit is love, joy, peace, longsuffering, kindness, goodness, faithfulness, (23) gentleness, self-control. Against such there is no law." (Galatians 5:16-18, 22-23 NKJV)

And Paul brings the discussion back to the Gospel, back to the Cross:

"And those who are Christ's have crucified the flesh with its passions and desires. (25) If we live in the Spirit, let us also walk in the Spirit." (Galatians 5:24-25 NKJV)

Consider for a moment what it means to be crucified: you cannot crucify yourself – impossible. You end up with a free hand. Jesus had to yield Himself to the Father's will and allow sinful men to crucify Him. So, it is with us; we surrender ourselves and let the Lord crucify us to Himself.

Question 1: How have you come to the place in your Christian life that you can say, "I am crucified with Christ!"
☐ Yes, by God's grace, I can say, "I am crucified with Christ!"
☐ Yes and no. I still struggle with my flesh and fail too often.
☐ No, I have no idea what "I am crucified with Christ!" means.

Let's look at the eighth quality of the Fruit of the Spirit: Gentleness.
  We are going to look at three areas in this lesson:

- We will look at the Bible and define the word gentleness.
- We will look at an illustration from the Old Testament showing gentleness.
- We will look at Jesus and the Cross' demonstration of gentleness.

What does Gentleness mean?
There is a family of Greek words that are used with our word in this lesson. In our text in Galatians 5:23, it is translated as:

Gentleness: NKJV; NLT; NIV; ESV; CSB; NASB; NET; RSV; HVN; AMP
Meekness: KJV; YLT; ASV; DBY; WEB; Wuest
πραότης, (**G4236**) prah-ot'-ace
KJV – meekness (9x) **Textus Receptus**
πρᾷος (**G4235**) prah'-os used in Matthew 11:29
πραΰτης (**G4240**) prah-oo'-tace
NASB – meekness (11x) Morphological GNT
πραΰς (**G4239**) prah-ooce' used in Matthew 5:5

Gentleness or Meekness means:

the mildness of temperament, the gentleness of spirit, by implication: humility

The word has the idea of being teachable, not having a superior attitude, not demanding one's rights.

Gentleness or meekness is humble *submissiveness* to the teachings of Divine revelation – this stands in contrast with that self-reliant, headstrong, impulsive person who is apt to hurry the adoption of novel ideas. This impulsive person has not taken the trouble seriously to weigh ideas in light of God's word. Gentleness or meekness, however, stands in contrast to self-reliant arrogance in general.

– *meekness* ("gentle strength"), which exercises *power* with *reserve and gentleness*.

This gentleness or meekness is both an inward quality of character and shows itself outwardly in our interactions with others. Gentleness or meekness is a work of the Holy Spirit and not of human will.

Question 2: How would you define "gentleness" in your own words?

So, let's look first at the:

Inward quality of a gentle or meek character:

Meekness toward God is that disposition of spirit in which we accept His dealings with us as useful, and therefore without disputing or resisting. In the OT, the meek are those wholly relying on God rather than their strength to defend against injustice. We saw Joseph show this kind of meekness and gentleness toward his brothers.

> *"Joseph said to them, "Do not be afraid, for am I in the place of God? (20) "But as for you, you meant evil against me; but God meant it for good, in order to bring it about as it is this day, to save many people alive." (Genesis 50:19-20 NKJV)*

Moses was described as meek (KJV) or humble when being attacked by Miriam and Aaron. God's testimony:

> *"(Now the man Moses was very humble, more than all men who were on the face of the earth.)" (Numbers 12:3 NKJV)*

This meek humility is found in the attitude of thankfulness:

> *"...in everything give thanks; for this is the will of God in Christ Jesus for you." (1 Thessalonians 5:18 NKJV)*

As we make our focus on Jesus and the Cross, recognizing His sovereign control of all things in life – we can and ought to humbly submit with thankfulness.

Meekness is not weakness! Biblical meekness (4236/*praótēs*) shows *God-paced, God-defined* behavior which acts *as the Lord Jesus acts*, i.e., Gentleness or meekness does not "act out" ("flying off the handle" with *human-based* anger.

> *"Let this mind be in you which was also in Christ Jesus." (Philippians 2:5 NKJV).*

We will come back later to Philippians 2.

"Blessed are the meek, for they shall inherit the earth." (Matthew 5:5 NKJV)

It is the gentle submissiveness to the divine will in all of life. This meekness is a qualify of faith and believing unto salvation.

"Therefore, lay aside all filthiness and overflow of wickedness, and receive with meekness the implanted word, which is able to save your souls." (James 1:21 NKJV)

Question 3: How has the Lord worked this fruit of gentleness or meekness in your life? What circumstances has the Lord used to humble you?

Let's look at the outward quality of gentleness:

Outward quality of gentleness or meekness toward others:

First to "evil" people:
This meekness then toward evil people means knowing God is permitting the injuries they inflict, that He uses them to purify His elect, and that He will deliver His elect in His time.

"The eyes of the LORD are on the righteous, And His ears are open to their cry. (16) The face of the LORD is against those who do evil, To cut off the remembrance of them from the earth. (17) The righteous cry out, and the LORD hears, And delivers them out

of all their troubles. (18) The LORD is near to those who have a broken heart, And saves such as have a contrite spirit. (19) Many are the afflictions of the righteous, But the LORD delivers him out of them all." (Psalm 34:15-19 NKJV)

Meekness - Πραοτης· Mildness, indulgence toward the weak and erring, patient suffering of injuries without feeling a spirit of revenge, an even balance of all tempers and passions, the entire opposite to anger.

Again Joseph, Moses, Paul, and especially Jesus are models of this meekness and gentleness. And Jesus is not only the model – but He is the source of that meekness and gentleness. We will find this is where the power comes from.

Question 4: How have you responded to "evil" people when they have wrongly accused or used you?

_____

_____

_____

_____

_____

The qualities of mildness, gentleness, and meekness in dealing with an erring brother:
avoids unnecessary harshness – yet without compromising or being slow to use necessary force.

Righteous Anger: Example of Jesus and the money changers. Jesus did not call out ten legions of angels. (Matthew 21:12-17; Mark 11:15-19; Luke 19:45-48; John 2:13-17). It was the zeal for the Father (not for Himself) that motivated Him.

Gentleness or meekness is not petty nor vindictive. Gentleness often requires laying aside "personal rights."

4236/*praotēs* ("gentle-force") refers to *temperate* behavior – divinely-balanced (*regulated by the Lord*), which avoids two problems: *negative* (personal) anger *and* the *sin of angerlessness*.

> "*Be angry, and do not sin*": *do not let the sun go down on your wrath*" (*Ephesians 4:26 NKJV*)

Biblical meekness is the opposite of a "clutching" (grabbing) spirit that displays anger because "you were offended, or someone upset you."

The meek - Meekness is patience in the reception of injuries. It is neither meanness nor a surrender of our rights, nor cowardice, but it is the opposite of sudden anger, of malice, of long-harbored vengeance. Christ insisted on his right when he said,

> "*If I have spoken evil, bear witness of the evil; but if well, why do you strike Me?*" (*John 18:23 NKJV*)

This powerful combination of the reserve (gentleness) and strength operates as *the risen Christ Himself lives through the believer* by the indwelling Holy Spirit.

Remember: The very next verses after the list of the fruit of the Spirit say:

> "*And those who are Christ's have crucified the flesh with its passions and desires. (25) If we live in the Spirit, let us also walk in the Spirit. (26) Let us not become conceited, provoking one another, envying one another.*" (*Galatians 5:24-26 NKJV*)

Then look at what Paul says next:

> "*Brethren, if a man is overtaken in any trespass, you who are spiritual restore such a one in a spirit of gentleness (G4236), considering yourself lest you also be tempted. (2) Bear one another's burdens, and so fulfill the law of Christ.*" (*Galatians 6:1-2 NKJV*)

Listen and see how we are to respond to those who have errored or sinned:

"in humility (gentleness/meekness - G4236) correcting those who are in opposition, if God perhaps will grant them repentance, so that they may know the truth" (*2 Timothy 2:25 NKJV*)

"with all lowliness and gentleness (G4236), with longsuffering, bearing with one another in love" (*Ephesians 4:2 NKJV*)

"to speak evil of no one, to be peaceable, gentle, showing all humility (gentleness/meekness) (G4236) to all men." (*Titus 3:2 NKJV*)

"But sanctify the Lord God in your hearts, and always be ready to give a defense to everyone who asks you a reason for the hope that is in you, with meekness and fear;" (*1 Peter 3:15 NKJV*)

Question 5: Do you see this gentleness or meekness when you are in disagreement between brothers? How do you see this fruit in bringing reconciliation to offended parties?

Let's consider the Holy Spirit working in our lives:

The work of the Holy Spirit growing gentleness or meekness to those crucified with Christ

Gentleness or meekness is the opposite of self-assertiveness and self-interest. It stems from trusting in God's goodness and control over the situation and your life. The gentle person is not occupied with self at all. This meekness is a work of the Holy Spirit, not of the human will; it is the one who has been crucified with Christ.

Gentleness is something that cannot be accomplished by self – nor is it merely "biological" (naturally patient or "laid back").

Never self-effort – only by the Cross.

> *"I have been crucified with Christ; it is no longer I who live, but Christ lives in me; and the life which I now live in the flesh I live by faith in the Son of God, who loved me and gave Himself for me. (21) "I do not set aside the grace of God; for if righteousness comes through the law, then Christ died in vain." (Galatians 2:20-21 NKJV*)

Gentleness is the kind of attitude that **<u>DOES NOT</u>** demand "its proper respect."

To paraphrase a quote by Spurgeon:

> *"What is the proper respect, which is due to poor creatures like us? I believe that if anyone of us did get our "proper respect," we should not like it long, for we would be found wanting on the scales of justice. We desire to be flattered when we cry out for 'proper respect.' Respect, indeed! It is not about you. Why, if we had our "proper respect" based on our thought, words, and actions, we would find ourselves to be in the lowest hell!"*

Humility and lowliness of mind, this gentleness, and meekness, of which Christ is an outstanding example and pattern. It is the Holy Spirit working in the heart of a regenerate person. It is not thinking ourselves more highly than we ought to think, but walking humbly with God, acknowledging every favor, being thankful for every blessing, and depending on his grace and behaving with modesty and humility among men.

Gentleness or meekness is to govern our passions and resentments, so as not to be easily provoked, and, when we are so, to be soon pacified,

"If then you were raised with Christ, seek those things which are above, where Christ is, sitting at the right hand of God. (2) Set your mind on things above, not on things on the earth. (3) For you died, and your life is hidden with Christ in God. ... (12) Therefore, as the elect of God, holy and beloved, put on tender mercies, kindness, humility, meekness, longsuffering; (13) bearing with one another, and forgiving one another, if anyone has a complaint against another; even as Christ forgave you, so you also must do." (Colossians 3:1-3, 12-13 NKJV)

Question 6: How have you been "bearing with one another" (especially those in your home) with a spirit of gentleness or meekness? Do you have a forgiving attitude, or do you hold a grudge?

Illustration: The Gentleness of God in the Garden

God in the garden after sin – **Genesis 3**

You know the story of our first parents and how sin entered into the world.

The Rule – just ONE rule!

"Then the LORD God took the man and put him in the garden of Eden to tend and keep it. (16) And the LORD God commanded the man, saying, "Of every tree of the garden you may freely eat; (17) "but of the tree of the knowledge of good and evil you shall not eat, for in the day that you eat of it you shall surely die." (Genesis 2:15-17 NKJV)

"And the LORD God said, "It is not good that man should be alone; I will make him a helper comparable to him." (Genesis 2:18 NKJV)

Then the Lord made every beast of the field and every bird of the air. Adam named the animals, but no helper comparable to Adam.

Deep sleep – took one rib – closed up the flesh. From the rib – made the woman.

Chapter 3 – The serpent spoke to the woman – he challenged the rule with a catechism question:

Q 1 - Has God indeed said: You shall not eat of every tree of the garden?
A 1 – We may eat the fruit of the trees of the garden; BUT of the fruit of the tree which is in the midst of the garden, God said, "You shall not eat it, nor shall you touch it, lest you die."

Oh, so close. But Eve or Adam added a "rule" to God's one rule.

"So when the woman saw that the tree was good for food, that it was pleasant to the eyes, and a tree desirable to make one wise, she took of its fruit and ate. She also gave to her husband with her, and he ate." (Genesis 3:6 NKJV)

They ate – eyes opened – naked – fig leaves to cover. Heard God coming, HIDE!

"Then the LORD God called to Adam and said to him, "Where are you?" (Genesis 3:9 NKJV)

What tone of voice do you hear? **"Where are you?"**

Disgust and contempt – How could you do this? How dare you. I gave you all this, and you do this to Me?. You disgust Me. "Where are you?"

Anger and wrath – Get out here, right this minute. You are in BIG trouble. "Where are you?"

Joyful, Laughter, and play – Oh, you silly children, ha-ha – are we playing "Hide and Seek?" "Where are you?" – here, I come ready or not.

Gentleness and compassion – Oh, Adam, what have you done? Where are you in a relationship with Me now?

Adam's response: It was all about self – ME:

> *So he said, "I heard Your voice in the garden (then came these emotions), and I was afraid (fear) because I was naked (guilt); and I hid myself (shame)." (Genesis 3:10 NKJV)*

Question 7: When you sin, do you ever feel fear, guilt, and shame? How do you try and hide your sin from others and God?

_____

_____

_____

_____

Now starts the "Blame Game" – NOT ME – Adam blamed God for the woman. The woman blamed the serpent.

There were a terrible judgment and curse following our first parents' sin. God cursed the serpent – with a promise – The Seed of the woman will crush the serpent's head, and the serpent will bruise His heel. (Genesis 3:15)

God's judgment on the woman multiply sorrow and pain in childbirth, and your husband will rule over you.

God's judgment on the man, the ground (the whole planet) is cursed, now he will work for his food by working the ground. And in the end, he will die and turn back into dust. And in Adam, we are now all cursed with his sin. His sin now becomes our sin.

But notice what God does next:

> *"Also, for Adam and his wife, the LORD God made tunics (garments, coats) of skin, and clothed them." (Genesis 3:21 NKJV)*

As the Lord kills these animals – this is a picture of the Father bringing His Son to be sacrificed for us.

This sacrifice will be the first of many sacrifices that will be offered - the innocent to pay for the guilty. It would be only a matter of time that Jesus will become that Lamb of God – to cover us with His blood and righteousness.

Question 8: How do you see a picture of the sacrifice on the Cross in Genesis 3:21? How does the innocent being slain and the guilty being clothed by the skin of the innocent parallel what Jesus did on the Cross?

Application: Jesus showing gentleness at the Cross

"Come to Me, all you who labor and are heavy laden, and I will give you rest. (29) "Take My yoke upon you and learn from Me, for I am gentle and lowly in heart, and you will find rest for your souls. (30) "For My yoke is easy and My burden is light." (Matthew 11:28-30 NKJV)

"Tell the daughter of Zion, 'Behold, your King is coming to you, Lowly, and sitting on a donkey, A colt, the foal of a donkey.'" (Matthew 21:5 NKJV)

"Now I, Paul, myself am pleading with you by the meekness and gentleness of Christ--who in presence am lowly among you, but being absent am bold toward you." (2 Corinthians 10:1 NKJV)

Read this description of Jesus' gentleness, meekness, and humility:

Who has believed our report? And to whom has the arm of the LORD been revealed? (2) For He shall grow up before Him as a tender plant, And as a root out of dry ground. He has no form or comeliness; And when we see Him, There is no beauty that we should desire Him. (3) He is despised and rejected by men, A Man of sorrows, and acquainted with grief. And we hid, as it were, our faces from Him; He was despised, and we did not esteem Him. (4) Surely He has borne our griefs And carried our sorrows; Yet we esteemed Him stricken, Smitten by God, and afflicted. (5) But He was wounded for our transgressions, He was bruised for our iniquities; The chastisement for our peace was upon Him, And by His stripes we are healed. (6) All we like sheep have gone astray; We have turned, every one, to his own way; And the LORD has laid on Him the iniquity of us all. (7) He was oppressed, and He was afflicted, Yet He opened not His mouth; He was led as a lamb to the slaughter, And as a sheep before its shearers is silent, So He opened not His mouth. (Isaiah 53:1-7 NKJV)

Paul paints a picture of this quality of gentleness or meekness in Philippians 2 – Jesus humbled Himself at the Cross:

"Therefore if there is any consolation in Christ, if any comfort of love, if any fellowship of the Spirit, if any affection and mercy, (2) fulfill my joy by being like-minded, having the same love, being of one accord, of one mind. (3) Let nothing be done through selfish ambition or conceit, but in lowliness of mind let each esteem others better than himself. (4) Let each of you look out not only for his own interests, but also for the interests of others. (5) Let this mind be in you which was also in Christ Jesus, (6) who, being in the form of God, did not consider it robbery to be equal with God, (7) but made Himself of no reputation, taking the form of a bondservant, and coming in the likeness of men. (8) And being found in appearance as a man, He humbled Himself and became obedient to the point of death, even the death of the cross. (9)

Therefore God also has highly exalted Him and given Him the name which is above every name, (10) that at the name of Jesus every knee should bow, of those in heaven, and of those on earth, and of those under the earth, (11) and that every tongue should confess that Jesus Christ is Lord, to the glory of God the Father." (*Philippians 2:1-11 NKJV*)

Question 9: How do you see Jesus humbling Himself there at the Cross? Have you considered this fruit of the Spirit comes from Jesus as He is crucified for your sins?

_____

_____

_____

_____

_____

"But we all, with unveiled face, beholding as in a mirror the glory of the Lord, are being transformed into the same image from glory to glory, just as by the Spirit of the Lord." (*2 Corinthians 3:18 NKJV*)

Self-control

As we look at this last characteristic of the fruit of the Spirit – remember the context is the battle going on within the Christian.

> *"I say then: Walk in the Spirit, and you shall not fulfill the lust of the flesh. (17) For the flesh lusts against the Spirit, and the Spirit against the flesh; and these are contrary to one another, so that you do not do the things that you wish." (Galatians 5:16-18 NKJV)*

After listing the works of the flesh and the nine qualities of the fruit, Paul brings the discussion back to the Gospel, back to the Cross:

> *"And those who are Christ's have crucified the flesh with its passions and desires. (25) If we live in the Spirit, let us also walk in the Spirit." (Galatians 5:24-25 NKJV)*

Let's look at the ninth and last quality of the Fruit of the Spirit: Self-control.

Walking in the Spirit in Self-control

- How does the Bible define and use self-control?
- An illustration from the Old Testament showing self-control
- How did Jesus at the Cross demonstrate self-control?

We find our word translated with two words:
Temperance: KJV; YLT; WEB
Self-control: NKJV; NLT; NIV; ESV; CSB; NASB; NET; RSV; AMP
"temperance" is now limited to one form of "self-control" of staying away

from alcohol or referring mainly to abstinence from intoxicating drinks. That is not the idea of this word - abstaining from alcohol.

"self-control" is commonly defined as the virtue of one who masters his desires and passions, esp. his sensual appetites; the ability to control oneself, particularly one's emotions and desires, especially in difficult situations. The ability to regulate one's feelings, thoughts, and behavior in the face of temptations and impulses. Synonyms: self-discipline, self-restraint, self-mastery, will power.

Wait a minute: It has been the Holy Spirit who has been working in our lives to bring forth love, joy, peace, longsuffering, kindness, goodness, faithfulness, gentleness – Now it's my turn to control myself? – Is this the idea of "self-control" here in **Galatians 5:23**?

Am I responsible for this ninth part of the fruit (11.11%)? Is "self-control" merely my self-discipline, my self-restraint, my self-mastery, my willpower.? That doesn't sound right.

Let's look at this Greek word more closely.

ἐγκράτεια **enkráteia**, eng-krat'-i-ah; (G1468) is a compound word:

from 1722/*en*, "*in* the sphere of"

and 2904/*krátos*, "dominion, mastery, power")

This sphere of *dominion,* strength, or power is from *within.* - This "self-control" is proceeding out from *within* oneself, **BUT** *not by the power and will of oneself.*

The sense here of **enkráteia** is that the Holy Spirit's influence on the heart makes a person moderate in all indulgences. The Holy Spirit teaches them to restrain their passions, govern themselves, control their evil propensities, and subdue all inordinate affection because they walk in the Spirit and not fulfill the flesh's lust.

So, the proper use of this Greek word stresses the controlling power of the will is under the operation of the Spirit of God; Jesus expressed this in His prayer:

"…saying, "Father, if it is Your will, take this cup away from Me; nevertheless not My will, but Yours, be done." (Luke 22:42 NKJV)

Question 1: How have you thought of "self-control" in the past? How does the fact that the Holy Spirit will be helping you in this area of your life?

_____

_____

_____

_____

_____

The Gospel Power

This "**enkráteia**" is the idea that my will is under the control of the Holy Spirit. For the believer, this control of the will or choice is brought under the Lord's power, submission, and control. And where does this power come from? The Gospel:

> *"For I am not ashamed of the Gospel of Christ, for it is the power of God to salvation for everyone who believes, for the Jew first and also for the Greek. (17) For in it the righteousness of God is revealed from faith to faith; as it is written, "The just shall live by faith." (Romans 1:16-17 NKJV)*

The Gospel is for salvation and our sanctification – as we live from faith to faith. We live the entirety of our Christian life by faith. To everyone who believes the Gospel personally (Jesus' death, burial, and resurrection) has this power to live the Christian life. That power is found in the daily application of the Gospel.

> *"For the message of the Cross is foolishness to those who are perishing, but to us who are being saved, it is the power of God."*
> *(1 Corinthians 1:18 NKJV)*

Again, the power of God is found in the message of the Cross. When we choose to look at ANY CIRCUMSTANCE from the view of the Cross, we find Godly;

Spirit-empowered, self-control. I come to the Cross to be washed from my sins, I come to the Cross and see the resurrection to live as I walk in the Spirit, I come to the Cross to take my stand in this battle against my sinful flesh.

As we are transformed more and more into the image of Christ (as we are in His workmanship), we find our time in the Word and prayer to be sweet.

> *"But we all, with unveiled face, beholding as in a mirror the glory of the Lord, are being transformed into the same image from glory to glory, just as by the Spirit of the Lord."* (*2 Corinthians 3:18 NKJV*)

As we gaze upon the glory of the Lord, we will be transformed into that same image from glory to glory. How does this happen? By the Spirit of the Lord as we spend time in the Word and prayer. And what is the glory of the Lord?

> *"The city had no need of the sun or of the moon to shine in it, for the glory of God illuminated it. The Lamb is its light."* (*Revelation 21:23 NKJV*)

The glory of God is found in the Lamb. The Lamb of God who takes away the sin of the world. (John 1:29)

We see that glory at the Cross.

Question 2: Why is it important to be in the Bible, seeing the Power of God contained in the Gospel?

Listen to the Holy Spirit

This "self-control" is a "Spirit-empowered" will power. As we read "self-control," – think "Spirit-empowered self-control." It is **NOT ME** controlling my will. It is the Holy Spirit – leading and directing with that still small voice that says, "This is the way – walk in it" (Isaiah 30:21), and we listen to the Holy Spirit.

> *"I will give you a new heart and put a new spirit within you; I will take the heart of stone out of your flesh and give you a heart of flesh. (27) "I will put My Spirit within you and cause you to walk in My statutes, and you will keep My judgments and do them."* (*Ezekiel 36:26-27 NKJV*)

> *"I will bring the blind by a way they did not know; I will lead them in paths they have not known. I will make darkness light before them, And crooked places straight. These things I will do for them, And not forsake them."* (*Isaiah 42:16 NKJV*)

> *"Thus says the LORD, your Redeemer, The Holy One of Israel: "I am the LORD your God, Who teaches you to profit, Who leads you by the way you should go."* (*Isaiah 48:17 NKJV*)

> *"Good and upright is the LORD; Therefore, He teaches sinners in the way. (9) The humble He guides in justice, And the humble He teaches His way."* (*Psalm 25:8-9 NKJV*)

> *"I will instruct you and teach you in the way you should go; I will guide you with My eye."* (*Psalm 32:8 NKJV*)

As we spend personal time in God's Word, as we spend personal time in our prayer closets – the Lord, by the Spirit within every believer, will lead and guide you to walk in the Spirit and not fulfill the lust of the flesh. As we humbly yield our wills by acknowledging our crucifixion to the Lord – we begin to exhibit that last quality of a "Spirit-empowered self-control."

Question 3: How would you describe the difference between "self-control" and "Spirit-empowered self-control?"

_____

_____

_____

_____

_____

_____

I want to look at every instance of the word "**enkráteia**" used in the New Testament. It is only four times in three verses in the Bible:

> *"And after some days, when Felix came with his wife Drusilla, who was Jewish, he sent for Paul and heard him concerning the faith in Christ. (25) Now, as he reasoned about righteousness, self-control* **(enkráteia)**, *and the judgment to come, Felix was afraid and answered, "Go away for now; when I have a convenient time, I will call for you." (26) Meanwhile, he also hoped that money would be given him by Paul, that he might release him. Therefore, he sent for him more often and conversed with him."* (Acts 24:24-26 NKJV)

While in prison in Caesarea, Paul had the opportunity to witness to Felix concerning the faith in Christ. As Felix listened concerning the righteousness found at the Cross, the changed life of a Spirt empowered "self-control," and the final judgment before a Holy God – Felix was afraid. Yet, for the hope of a bribe (which Paul would not do), Paul witnessed to Felix often and conversed with him over two years while Paul remained in prison.

We find the second use of this word in:

> *"But the fruit of the Spirit is love, joy, peace, longsuffering, kindness, goodness, faithfulness, (23) gentleness, self-control* **(enkráteia)**. *Against such there is no law."* (Galatians 5:22-23 NKJV)

Here we have our "Spirit-empowered self-control" as the ninth part of the fruit. Remember, these aspects of the fruit are a "blend of flavors."

So, the love, joy, peace, longsuffering, kindness, goodness, faithfulness, and gentleness are displayed in Spirit-empowered self-control.

The Spirit-empowered self-control will say **NO** to the works of the flesh: **NO** to:

> "adultery, fornication, uncleanness, lewdness, (20) idolatry, sorcery, hatred, contentions, jealousies, outbursts of wrath, selfish ambitions, dissensions, heresies, (21) envy, murders, drunkenness, revelries, and the like." (Galatians 5:19-21 NKJV)

When we are tempted to sin – the Spirit-empowered self-control says **NO!**

Question 4: How much hope does this give you? That by the power of the Holy Spirit, working through the Gospel message of Jesus' death, burial, and resurrection, you can say, "NO!" to temptations.

The last verses where this word "**enkráteia**" is used:

> "But also for this very reason, giving all diligence, add to your faith virtue, to virtue knowledge, (6) to knowledge self-control (**enkráteia**), to self-control (**enkráteia**) perseverance, to perseverance godliness, (7) to godliness brotherly kindness, and to brotherly kindness love. (8) For if these things are yours and abound, you will be neither barren nor unfruitful in the knowledge of our Lord Jesus Christ." (2 Peter 1:5-8 NKJV)

For the believer, **enkráteia** ("Spirit-empowered self-control") is only accomplished *by the power of the risen Lord through faith*. It is not by "self-will."

Question 5: Are you beginning to see that "self-control" is only achieved by coming to the Cross and your faith walk in the Spirit?
- ☐ Yes, I believe it is only by faith in the finished work of the Cross will I have the power to walk in the Spirit.
- ☐ I'm still struggling to understand the idea of walking in the Spirit by faith.
- ☐ No, I believe I can do this without any help from the Holy Spirit.

It is by Faith
("Holy Spirit dominion from within") ("Spirit-empowered self-control") results from *Christ* speaking His "*rhēma*-word" of faith *in* the heart of the believer – Remember, we talked about this faith/faithfulness a few weeks ago.

> *"So then faith comes by hearing, and hearing by the word of God."*
> (*Romans 10:17 NKJV*)

This faith is persuading us of His will for our lives. This faith gives the power we need to do His will – from the inside out!

In summary, **enkráteia** ("Spirit-empowered self-control") is *Spirit*-directed and *Spirit*-empowered, *fruit of the Holy Spirit*. It results from personally knowing the risen Christ through the Word of God (the Bible) and prayer.

("Spirit-empowered self-control") only *operates by knowing the Master*! Jesus Christ *empowers* us to live *out* the faith He works *in us*, "through (His divine) love."

> *"I have been crucified with Christ; it is no longer I who live, but Christ lives in me; and the life which I now live in the flesh I live by faith in the Son of God, who loved me and gave Himself for me. (21) "I do not set aside the grace of God; for if righteousness comes through the law, then Christ died in vain." (Galatians 2:20-21 NKJV)*

Do not be confused by the "self-help" industry that sells billions of books to tell you that "you can achieve anything you put your mind to. Believe in yourself." We are told to read that "self-help" book and follow these steps. However, what is done in the flesh will not last. And sprinkling Bible verses over these man-made self-helps don't work either. We already have a "self-help" book – we call it "the Bible." We need to learn how to apply God's word to all of life.

The Christian life is not a set of rules to be followed to have success. Jesus clearly said,

"If you love Me, keep My commandments." (John 14:15 NKJV)

It does not say, "Keep My commandments, and I will love you." Because we love Jesus – we want to keep His commandments. So, Paul is showing us that as we are in this battle of the flesh – we come to the Cross, resting in the finished work of Christ. And daily, we remind ourselves – we are crucified with Christ.

Question 6: Fill in the blank: "_____ have been _____ with _____; it is no longer _____ who live, but _____ lives in me; and the life which I now live in the flesh _____ live by _____ in the Son of God, who loved _____ and gave Himself for _____." (Galatians 2:20 NKJV)

Illustration: An example of a "Spirit-empowered – self-controlled" life of David – the shepherd boy.

Who was David?
David is first mentioned at the end of the Book of Ruth. (A short book that illustrates and foreshadows Christ as our kinsmen redeemer.) And then how David is in the linage of God's promised Messiah. Then the next book in the Bible is 1 Samuel.

Saul, the first king of Israel, had been rejected by God because Saul turned his back from following the Lord and not performing the Lord's commandments. (1 Samuel 15:1-35)

Next chapter:

> *"Now the LORD said to Samuel, "How long will you mourn for Saul, seeing I have rejected him from reigning over Israel? Fill your horn with oil and go; I am sending you to Jesse the Bethlehemite. For I have provided Myself a king among his sons."* (*1 Samuel 16:1 NKJV*)

As Samuel starts going through the sons – oldest to youngest…

> *"But the LORD said to Samuel, "Do not look at his appearance or at his physical stature, because I have refused him. For the LORD does not see as man sees; for man looks at the outward appearance, but the LORD looks at the heart."* (*1 Samuel 16:7 NKJV*)

It is not until Samuel takes the horn of oil and anoints Jesse's youngest son that David's name is mentioned. (1 Samuel 16:13) David is secretly anointed to be the next king.

The story of David and Goliath
Next Chapter: I Samuel 17:1-58

We find David – resting in the Lord -> doing what is right. David will be demonstrating a "Spirit-empowered – self-controlled" life in meeting Goliath.

The Philistines gathered against Israel. Philistines stood on a mountain on one side, and Israel stood on a mountain on the other side with a valley between them.

Goliath was six cubits and a span tall (9' 6") Bronze helmet, bronze coat of mail: 150 to 200 lbs., spear like a weaver's beam with the iron spearhead of 18 lbs. Along with his armor-bearer holding his shield.

The challenge: Send one man to fight, and the winner takes all. "I defy the armies of Israel."

(**v 16**) forty days both morning and evening: Goliath keeps mocking God and challenging Israel. Israel was already defeated by fear.

Forty days reminds me of Jesus' temptations for 40 days – Satan, mocking God and challenging Jesus. (Matthew 4:1-11) (v 17-20) David was sent by his father – "check on your brothers." In the same way – Jesus was sent by His Father.

(v 26) David is viewing the "problem" from God's perspective: "For who is this uncircumcised Philistine, that he should defy the armies of the living God?" David kept up this question – And Saul heard this report.

"Then David said to Saul, "Let no man's heart fail because of him; your servant will go and fight with this Philistine." (1 Samuel 17:32 NKJV)

(v 34-37) David the good shepherd: fought a lion and a bear in protecting the sheep.

> *"Your servant has killed both lion and bear; and this uncircumcised Philistine will be like one of them, seeing he has defied the armies of the living God." (37) Moreover, David said, "The LORD, who delivered me from the paw of the lion and from the paw of the bear, He will deliver me from the hand of this Philistine." And Saul said to David, "Go, and the LORD be with you!" (1 Samuel 17:36-37 NKJV)*

David was a man after God's heart, who will do all of God's will: (Acts 13:22)
Psalm 63 – Notice David's focus and what consumed his thoughts.

> *"A Psalm of David when he was in the wilderness of Judah. O God, You are my God; Early will I seek You; My soul thirsts for You; My flesh longs for You In a dry and thirsty land Where there is no water. (2) So I have looked for You in the sanctuary, To see Your power and Your glory. (3) Because Your lovingkindness is better than life, My lips shall praise You." (Psalm 63:1-3 NKJV)*

The Lord consumed David's thoughts.

Question 7: What consumes your thoughts? What do you think about during the day?

_____

_____

_____

_____

_____

Personal illustration: What do you think about during the day? What do you fill your mind with during the day? I used to play games on the computer (a lot of games.) My thoughts were consumed by playing. It started while in seminary and had a "portable computer" that I brought to class. Kaypro – with a whopping 258k of memory and weighed about 20 lbs. I used these large 7.5-inch disks to save my work. I was able to play games on this computer. Later, I got better computers with the capacity to play more sophisticated games. The first version of WarCraft was a favorite.

I would be building a little kingdom to fight off bad guys. I spent hours, days, weeks, and months building my little kingdom. Later, as the internet became more accessible, I would go online and found a Christian group playing a game to beat "the boss." I enjoyed it a lot. I would set my alarm to get up in the middle of the night – because we had set a time to be together to "beat the next level." I was in bondage to this time waster – my thoughts were consumed with this gaming. I would justify this "Christian fellowship" and even share a daily bible verse that would encourage us in our gaming battles. I was in bondage in this.

These games were consuming my thoughts – but look at David – He was laser-focused on the Lord.

(v 40-50) David refused to wear Saul's armor to fight Goliath. With his sling and five stones – David approached Goliath, who asked: "Am I a dog, that you come to me with sticks?" And the Philistine cursed David by his gods. "Come to me, and I will give your flesh to the birds."

David responded:

"You come to me with a sword, a spear, and a javelin BUT I come in the name of the Lord of hosts, the God of the armies of Israel, whom you have defied." (1 Samuel 17:45 NKJV)

(v 48-50) As Goliath drew near to David – David ran toward the enemy army stationed on that mountain to meet this Philistine – he reached into his bag – took a stone and with his sling struck the giant in his forehead. The stone sank into his forehead and fell.

(v 50) The last part of verse 50 says:

"But there was no sword in the hand of David."

Don't miss this: Like Jesus would crush the serpent's head (Genesis 3:15) So, David crushed the giant's skull with a stone. But to make sure the giant was dead – David took Goliath's sword and cut off his head. David made sure Goliath was definitely dead by using Goliath's own weapon.

Consider how this points us to the Cross.

"Inasmuch then as the children have partaken of flesh and blood, He (Jesus) Himself likewise shared in the same, that through death He might destroy him who had the power (2904/krátos,) of death, that is, the devil," (Hebrews 2:14 NKJV)

David used Goliath's sword to kill him, so Jesus used the "power of death" [Satan's sword] (to be killed Himself and die on the Cross). The weapon of death Jesus used to destroy the devil. Then three days later – Jesus rose from the dead.

Satan bit off more than he could chew.

David's "self-control" was solely based upon his trusting and walking with the Lord. David looked at this situation from the Lord's perspective and not from a merely human perspective. David was not following some 12-step program of self-help to convince himself, "I can do this!"

"A Song of Ascents. I will lift up my eyes to the hills--From whence comes my help? (2) My help comes from the LORD, Who made heaven and earth." (Psalm 121:1-2 NKJV)

Yes, David maintained Spirit-empowered self-control that was focused on the Lord.

Question 8: How does this story of David and Goliath help you in reevaluating what you focus upon? What changes do you need to make to be more Cross focused?

_____

_____

_____

_____

_____

_____

Application: Jesus' self-control at the Cross
Jesus was always submitting to the Father. The Cross was always on Jesus' heart and mind. Jesus knew that He would be that final sacrifice for sin. Jesus was submitted to the Father's will.

> "Then Jesus answered and said to them, "Most assuredly, I say to you, the Son can do nothing of Himself, but what He sees the Father do; for whatever He does, the Son also does in like manner." (John 5:19 NKJV)

> "For I have come down from heaven, not to do My own will, but the will of Him who sent Me. (39) "This is the will of the Father who sent Me, that of all He has given Me I should lose nothing but should raise it up at the last day. (40) "And this is the will of Him who sent Me, that everyone who sees the Son and believes in Him may have everlasting life; and I will raise him up at the last day." (John 6:38-40 NKJV)

Jesus was preaching the Gospel (His death, burial, and resurrection) throughout His ministry.

"Jesus answered them and said, "My doctrine is not Mine, but His who sent Me." (*John 7:16 NKJV*)

"Then Jesus said to them, "When you lift up the Son of Man, then you will know that I am He, and that I do nothing of Myself; but as My Father taught Me, I speak these things." (*John 8:28 NKJV*) *(again, a reference to the Cross)*

"For I have not spoken on My own authority; but the Father who sent Me gave Me a command, what I should say and what I should speak." (*John 12:49 NKJV*)

"Do you not believe that I am in the Father and the Father in Me? The words that I speak to you I do not speak on My own authority; but the Father who dwells in Me does the works." (*John 14:10 NKJV*)

Question 9: What pattern do you see with Jesus? What is controlling Jesus' thinking?

_____

_____

_____

_____

Jesus demonstrated SELF-CONTROL in those last hours of His life on earth – Jesus never retaliated during His passion and was silent as a Lamb going to the slaughter there on the Cross. (**Isaiah 53**)

"For the grace of God that brings salvation has appeared to all men, (12) teaching us that, denying ungodliness and worldly lusts, we should live soberly, righteously, and godly in the present age, (13) looking for the blessed hope and glorious appearing of our great God and Savior Jesus Christ, (14) who gave Himself for us, that He might redeem us from every lawless deed and purify for Himself His own special people, zealous for good works." (Titus 2:11-14 NKJV)

This self-control is not you being in control of yourself. When you are walking in the Spirit, bearing the fruit of the Spirit, you will have a life empowered by the Holy Spirit that reflects Jesus.

"I can do all things through Christ who strengthens me." (Philippians 4:13 NKJV)

"But put on the Lord Jesus Christ, and make no provision for the flesh, to fulfill its lusts." (Romans 13:14 NKJV)

The personal illustration of my bondage to gaming on the computer, the Lord has freed me from that bondage. I had been studying the power of the Gospel here at Setting Captives Free. I was editing and reviewing some new lessons that would be offered with SCF 2.0. As I reviewed the course called: "Media Addiction," – I saw how bad my bondage to gaming was in my life. By a step of faith, I asked the Lord's forgiveness for all the wasted time over the years. I deleted all the games off my computer, my tablet, my phone. I even deleted the solitaire games. There were no more games – I experienced great relief, and a burden was lifted. I was free. This deleting my games was a Spirit-empowered self-controlled step of faith for me.

Now, I found I have an abundance of time to study God's word. I am involved in mentoring men through Setting Captives Free in the areas of life-dominating sins like pornography, gluttony, media addiction, depression, and helping men who desire to become mentors as they found real freedom from sin's bondage.

Am I still tempted to play games? Yes, but I quickly say, "No, thanks – I'm too busy with the Lord. Bye." This type of "self-control" only comes from the Spirit working in me.

Question 10: Are there things that need to be "deleted" in your life? What changes can you take that a "Spirit-empowered self-control can only do?"

We are finished looking at the fruit of the Spirit. The next few lessons will focus on Walking in the Spirit vs. fulfilling the lust of the flesh. Then look at what it means to put on the Lord Jesus and abide in Him.

Are You Walking in the Spirit or the Flesh?

> *"I say then: Walk in the Spirit, and you shall not fulfill the lust of the flesh. (17) For the flesh lusts against the Spirit, and the Spirit against the flesh; and these are contrary to one another, so that you do not do the things that you wish. (18) But if you are led by the Spirit, you are not under the law."* (*Galatians 5:16-18 NKJV*)

Walking in the Spirit or the Flesh?

- What does the Bible say about not gratifying the flesh?
- What illustration from the Old Testament?
- How does the Cross help us in this battle?

How not to gratify the flesh – Law vs. Faith

> *"I say then: Walk in the Spirit, and you shall not fulfill the lust of the flesh."* (*Galatians 5:16 NKJV*)

Usually, there have been three lines of thought on how not to gratify the flesh:

One: I must DO, DO, DO the Law, and obey God's word to achieve and maintain a right standing before God. I have been saved; now I must obey, keep, and do the Law to stay in a right relationship with God to be sanctified.

> *"The LORD your God will make you abound in all the work of your hand, in the fruit of your body, in the increase of your livestock, and in the produce of your land for good. For the LORD will again rejoice over you for good as He rejoiced over your fathers, (10) "if you obey the voice of the LORD your God, to keep His commandments and His statutes which are written in this Book of the Law, and if you turn to the LORD your God with all your heart and with all your soul."* (*Deuteronomy 30:9-10 NKJV*)

This was the position and teaching of the Pharisees: Notice how this thinking influenced the rich young ruler:

> "Now a certain ruler asked Him, saying, "Good Teacher, what shall I do to inherit eternal life?" (19) So, Jesus said to him, "Why do you call Me good? No one is good but One, that is, God. (20) "You know the commandments: 'Do not commit adultery,' 'Do not murder,' 'Do not steal,' 'Do not bear false witness,' 'Honor your father and your mother.' " (21) And he said, "All these things I have kept from my youth." (22) So when Jesus heard these things, He said to him, "You still lack one thing. Sell all that you have and distribute to the poor, and you will have treasure in heaven; and come, follow Me." (23) But when he heard this, he became very sorrowful, for he was very rich." (*Luke 18:18-23 NKJV*)

Jesus did not cover all Ten commandments – if he had – the answer from the ruler would have probably been different. But Jesus did address a covetous heart. He loved his riches more than willing to follow Jesus. The Law only brought one result: He was very sorrowful.

In the Sermon on the Mount – Jesus set the bar so high – it even included our thoughts breaking the Law.

We are unable to obey, keep, and do the Law perfectly. And that is the only standard that God will accept.

> "For whoever shall keep the whole law, and yet stumble in one point, he is guilty of all." (*James 2:10 NKJV*)

> "Therefore by the deeds of the law no flesh will be justified in His sight, for by the law is the knowledge of sin." (*Romans 3:20 NKJV*)

> "knowing that a man is not justified by the works of the law but by faith in Jesus Christ, even we have believed in Christ Jesus, that we might be justified by faith in Christ and not by the works of the law; for by the works of the law no flesh shall be justified." (*Galatians 2:16 NKJV*)

Oh, but the law is for our sanctification – not our justification. Is that what the Bible teaches? Paul quoted Jesus' words to him in his testimony before King Agrippa.

> "'I will deliver you from the Jewish people, as well as from the Gentiles, to whom I now send you, (18) 'to open their eyes, in order to turn them from darkness to light, and from the power of Satan to God, that they may receive forgiveness of sins and an inheritance among those who are sanctified by faith in Me.'" (*Acts 26:17-18 NKJV*)

After a list of sinful behaviors that were predominate in the lives of the people in Corinth, Paul writes to the church and says:

> "And such were some of you. But you were washed, but you were sanctified, but you were justified in the name of the Lord Jesus and by the Spirit of our God." (*1 Corinthians 6:11 NKJV*)

> "Therefore Jesus also, that He might sanctify the people with His own blood, suffered outside the gate." (*Hebrews 13:12 NKJV*)

> "O foolish Galatians! Who has bewitched you that you should not obey the truth before whose eyes Jesus Christ was clearly portrayed among you as crucified? (2) This only I want to learn from you: Did you receive the Spirit by the works of the law, or by the hearing of faith? (3) Are you so foolish? Having begun in the Spirit, are you now being made perfect by the flesh?" (*Galatians 3:1-3 NKJV*)

For further study:
  (John 17:17, 19; Romans 15:16; 2 Thessalonians 2:13)

Question 1: How have you tried to conquer your flesh by keeping the law in your own strength? How did that work for you?

How did Jesus address this "legalism" of the Pharisees?

> *"You search the Scriptures, for in them you think you have eternal life; and these are they which testify of Me. (40) "But you are not willing to come to Me that you may have life." (John 5:39-40 NKJV)*

The second way to think about "gratifying the flesh" is not to worry because if I'm saved – it doesn't make any difference – my sin is already forgiven.

Two: I can DO, DO, DO the sin - Because I have been saved, saved, saved and I do not need to be concerned about my sinning – in fact: Paul addressed this type of thinking several times:

> *"And why not say, "Let us do evil that good may come"?--as we are slanderously reported and as some affirm that we say. Their condemnation is just. ... (31) Do we then make void the law through faith? Certainly not! On the contrary, we establish the law." (Romans 3:8, 31 NKJV)*

> *"Moreover the law entered that the offense might abound. But where sin abounded, grace abounded much more, (21) so that as sin reigned in death, even so grace might reign through righteousness to eternal life through Jesus Christ our Lord. (1) What shall we say then? Shall we continue in sin that grace may abound?" (Romans 5:20-21; 6:1 NKJV)*

> *"Certainly not! How shall we who died to sin live any longer in it?"* (*Romans 6:2 NKJV*)

Of course, not; God forbid; By no means; Absolutely not; May it never be; let it not be; Far be the thought.

> *"What then? Shall we sin because we are not under law but under grace? Certainly not!"* (*Romans 6:15 NKJV*)

> *"For you, brethren, have been called to liberty; only do not use liberty as an opportunity for the flesh, but through love serve one another."* (*Galatians 5:13 NKJV*)

For further study:
    (1 Peter 2:16; Jude 1:4)

Question 2: Have you ever thought about gratifying your flesh and thinking that it is all covered by the blood? Picture yourself, standing under the Cross and sinning. What are you about thinking now?

_____

_____

_____

_____

_____

We have a word to define this type of person: antinomian (against law), the license to sin without eternal consequences. They are wrong, wrong, wrong.

Three: I can rest, rest, rest in the finished work of Jesus Christ on the Cross, because He DID, DID, DID the Law perfectly.

"Stand fast therefore in the liberty by which Christ has made us free, and do not be entangled again with a yoke of bondage." (*Galatians 5:1 NKJV*)

"and be found in Him, not having my own righteousness, which is from the law, but that which is through faith in Christ, the righteousness which is from God by faith;" (*Philippians 3:9 NKJV*)

"who has saved us and called us with a holy calling, not according to our works, but according to His own purpose and grace which was given to us in Christ Jesus before time began," (*2 Timothy 1:9 NKJV*)

Question 3: How can you come to the Cross and rest in the finished work of Jesus? In what practical ways can you rest?

I went down a "rabbit trail" as I looked up that word to "gratify" in Galatians 5:16. In Greek, it is **τελέσητε** comes from (τελέω teleo meaning to bring to a close, to finish, to perform and complete an action, should have fully developed.) This is the same word that Jesus used on the Cross when He said, *"It is finished."* (John 19:30) (That is something to be thinking about and reflecting upon.)

There on the Cross, Jesus brought to a close, completed an action, and finished the purpose that He came to do – to become the only sacrifice to die on a bloody Cross and pay in full the punishment of our sins that we deserved.

This verb **τελέσητε** in Galatians 5:16, (getting a bit technical here) is preceded by two negative words [οὐ no] and [μὴ not]. And, τελέσητε is an Aorist Active Subjunctive 2nd person verb form. What does this all mean? The Aorist is expressing that an action has happened and is ongoing, the Active voice (2nd person – you are doing this), and the Subjunctive is the idea of "likely to occur," but with the two negative words before it expresses a "double negative; the impossibility of an action to occur."

So, put this all together, if you are walking in the Spirit – it will be IMPOSSIBLE for you even to begin to gratify, fulfill, complete, perform the action, to finish the lust/desires of the flesh in sinning against God.

This is why this point of "Walking in the Spirit" is so important to understand and learn how to do this in these lessons. As we are walking in the Spirit – our total dependence and power are coming through the Cross, knowing we have been washed and continuing to be washing at the Cross by the blood of the Lamb.

We learn that we are given a new heart (Ezekiel 36:26-27) that our desire for loving God grows more than loving sin. Then because the power of the Gospel is given to us to live out our Christian life – we will be warring against the flesh as we continue to walk in the Spirit and find our only cleansing, hope, and power at the Cross.

Application for me: when I am yielding to gratify the flesh – I am not walking in the Spirit. It is impossible to be doing both at the same time. It is either I am walking in the Spirit or gratifying the flesh. So, for me, when those desires of the flesh are active, I need to stop and run to the Cross and sit there and look up at my Savior and Lord until my thoughts have been washed; I am again walking with the Spirit by faith and ready to start warring against my flesh and to crucify it to the Cross.

Question 4: What are some things you need to be doing to help you with your walking in the Spirit? How do you understand that you are either walking in the Spirit or gratifying the flesh?

Walking in the Spirit: Illustration from life

Rusty and his gait belt

A student from Setting Captives Free asked, "How do I walk in the Spirit, so I don't fall?"

I thought: "Good question."

On the weekends, I used to work with my friend Rusty, a 58-year-old gentleman who needed 24-hour care. He was VERY unstable on his feet and required a gait belt around the house or wheelchair for long distances. I used the gait belt with Rusty to help him walk from point A to point B in the house

- he was very fearful of falling. I had to come alongside behind him with my right hand securely hanging on to the gait belt in the middle of his back, my left hand supporting his left hand. My body was next to his, and I walked with "his gait," yet I was keeping his center of gravity over his feet while guiding him in the direction he was to go.

I was also telling Rusty, "It's okay; I won't let you fall because friends don't let friends fall." And I was instructing Rusty where we were going, like the toilet, or his favorite chair to watch TV, etc. I also had to remind Rusty not to get up on his own, like when he was on the toilet, because, at times, he would get up and start walking and would always fall. He would take a few steps - panic - and fall. He had his "free will," and at times, he used it without me. I had to be at arm's reach and be able to "catch him" before he fell.

I think it is that way with us. By ourselves - we will fall - but the Holy Spirit is there who comes alongside, holding us up and telling us - *"this is the way, walk in it."*

Jesus uses this image when calling the Holy Spirit, our Helper, Advocate, Comforter, Counselor. (John 14:16,26; 15:26 and 16:7)

The Greek word is: (παράκλητος paráklētos: summoned, called to one's side, esp. called to one's aid, in the widest sense, a helper, aider, assistant, advocate lawyer.)

The Holy Spirit was destined to take the place of Christ with the apostles (after his ascension to the Father), to lead them to a deeper knowledge of the gospel truth and give them divine strength needed to enable them to undergo trials and persecutions on behalf of the kingdom of God.

When I am listening, the Holy Spirit walks with "my gait" but keeps my "center of gravity" over my feet while guiding me in the direction He wants me to go. Then He reminds me - "Don't get up without Me." But at times, I get up, take a few steps on my own, and it is only a matter of time I find that I have fallen. When Rusty fell, I didn't scold him for disobeying me; I gently reassured him that he was okay; I picked him up and helped set him back down where he should be.

I had been working with Rusty for many years – when I first wrote this response, it was the first time I saw how the Lord had been caring for me like I had been caring for Rusty. The only difference was Rusty listened to me more than I had been listening to the Lord. By God's grace - I'm going to let the Lord grab hold of my "gait belt" before I get up.

I can do all things through Christ. Is it I or Christ? If you could have asked Rusty – he thought he was doing the walking – but he would fall and be helpless to get up without me.

Question 5: What do you need to do to let the Holy Spirit grab your "Gait belt?"

When we are walking in the Spirit – we are walking with God, we are walking with Jesus.

> *"They also do no iniquity; They walk in His ways." (Psalm 119:3 NKJV)*

> *"Your ears shall hear a word behind you, saying, "This is the way, walk in it," Whenever you turn to the right hand Or whenever you turn to the left." (Isaiah 30:21 NKJV)*

> *"Thus says the LORD: "Stand in the ways and see, And ask for the old paths, where the good way is, And walk in it; Then you will find rest for your souls. But they said, 'We will not walk in it.'" (Jeremiah 6:16 NKJV)*

> *"For you were once darkness, but now you are light in the Lord. Walk as children of light." (Ephesians 5:8 NKJV)*

For further study:
    (Psalm 143:8; Proverbs 28:26; Romans 8:1-4; Romans 13:13; Ephesians 2:2; Colossians 1:10)

"Let not mercy and truth forsake you; Bind them around your neck, Write them on the tablet of your heart, (4) And so find favor and high esteem In the sight of God and man. (5) Trust in the LORD with all your heart, And lean not on your own understanding; (6) In all your ways acknowledge Him, And He shall direct your paths. (7) Do not be wise in your own eyes; Fear the LORD and depart from evil." (*Proverbs 3:3-7 NKJV*)

Question 6: How are you, "writing God's word on the tablet of your heart?" How will this help in walking in the Spirit?

_____

_____

_____

_____

_____

Let's look at an OT illustration that exemplifies this Proverb - the application of walking in the Spirit and not fulfilling the lust of the flesh:

Old Testament illustration:
Joseph in Potiphar's house – **Genesis 39**

You remember Joseph's story and how he was a type of Christ who suffered at the hands of his brothers, sold into slavery, but by God's hand became second in command of Egypt. Because of his position there at the right hand of Pharaoh – he was able to save his family and the nation of Egypt.

I want to focus a moment on Joseph's trials while in Potiphar's house.

Potiphar, an officer of Pharaoh, captain of the guard – bought Joseph.

The Lord was with Joseph and blessed everything he did in Potiphar's house. Potiphar saw how everything Joseph did prospered. He really liked Joseph and made him the overseer of his house, and everyone was under Joseph's authority. Potiphar so trusted Joseph that he didn't even know what he had going on in his house, except that was served at mealtime. "I have no idea what is going on in my house – but this food is great."

Verse 6 says that Joseph was handsome in form and appearance.

In comes the temptation, Potiphar's wife.

Potiphar's wife (no name ever is given) – lusted after Joseph – "come to bed with me." Notice Joseph's response: "How can I do this great wickedness and sin against God?"

Day after day, she kept asking, "Come to bed with me." Joseph avoided her like the Covid and maintained his social distancing. Until one day – when all others were out of the house – she grabbed his coat – "Come to bed with me!" – Joseph peeled out of his coat and ran out of the house.

She cried out, "RAPE." And we know the rest of the story – prison for Joseph.

"It is better to lose a good coat than a good conscience." (Matthew Henry)

Do you see how Jesus also was tempted and responded? We get a glimpse of the temptation in **Matthew 4** and **Luke 4**. 40 days in fasting and prayer – the devil tempts Jesus in food, in covetousness, in pride. Lust of the flesh, the lust of the eyes, and the pride of life. (1 John 2:16) Each time Jesus did not argue or reason – but quoted an applicable verse from God's word to counter the temptation. "It is written…" "How can I do this great wickedness and sin against God?"

Question 7: Are you so filled with God's word – that as you are walking in the Spirit – God's word comes to mind? Are you hearing – "This is the way – walk in it – and run-away!"? How can you have this type of mindset on God's word?

Jesus maintained His sinless life for our sake.

Application: of the Cross – Look at Jesus
Our High Priest tempted

> *"For we do not have a High Priest who cannot sympathize with our weaknesses, but was in all points tempted as we are, yet without sin." (Hebrews 4:15 NKJV)*

> *"Therefore, in all things He had to be made like His brethren, that He might be a merciful and faithful High Priest in things pertaining to God, to make propitiation (appeasing God's wrath) for the sins of the people. (18) For in that He Himself has suffered, being tempted, He is able to aid those who are tempted." (Hebrews 2:17-18 NKJV)*

> *"And you know that He was manifested to take away our sins, and in Him there is no sin." (1 John 3:5 NKJV)*

For further study:
(Isaiah 53:9; Luke 22:28; 2 Corinthians 5:21; Hebrews 7:26 NKJV)
Yes, but Jesus…. Yes, we are tempted, But we can run to Jesus.

"Therefore let him who thinks he stands take heed lest he fall. (13) No temptation has overtaken you except such as is common to man; but God is faithful, who will not allow you to be tempted beyond what you are able, but with the temptation will also make the way of escape, that you may be able to bear it." (1 Corinthians 10:12-13 NKJV)

How can we escape? Like Joseph, we run to the Cross. In Christ Jesus, we can…

Question 8: How can you find "the way to escape" these temptations in your daily walk? How can you turn to the Cross to find God's faithfulness?

Did Jesus live like this?

"How can a young man cleanse his way? By taking heed according to Your word. (10) With my whole heart I have sought You; Oh, let me not wander from Your commandments! (11) Your word I have hidden in my heart, That I might not sin against You. (12) Blessed are You, O LORD! Teach me Your statutes. (13) With my lips I have declared All the judgments of Your mouth. (14) I have rejoiced in the way of Your testimonies, As much as in all riches. (15) I will meditate on Your precepts, And contemplate Your ways. (16) I will delight myself in Your statutes; I will not forget Your word." (Psalm 119:9-16 NKJV)

Jesus fulfilled this perfectly – now "in Him" we too can fulfill this Psalm in Christ.

"He who says he abides in Him ought himself also to walk just as He walked." (1 John 2:6 NKJV)

"Come to Me, all you who labor and are heavy laden, and I will give you rest. (29) "Take My yoke upon you and learn from Me, for I am gentle and lowly in heart, and you will find rest for your souls. (30) "For My yoke is easy and My burden is light." (Matthew 11:28-30 NKJV)

Question 9: How have you yoked up with Jesus? How are you walking with Him step by step?

Being Fruitful

*W*e come to the end of this series. I want us to look at one more thing concerning the fruit of the Spirit. And ask you, "Are you being fruitful?"

> *"But the fruit of the Spirit is love, joy, peace, longsuffering, kindness, goodness, faithfulness, (23) gentleness, self-control. Against such there is no law. (24) And those who are Christ's have crucified the flesh with its passions and desires. (25) If we live in the Spirit, let us also walk in the Spirit."* (*Galatians 5:22-25 NKJV*)

The fruit of the Spirit comes through the Cross as we are crucified with Christ. We live in the Spirit by God's grace and walk in the Spirit.

In this lesson, we will look at:

- What does the Bible say about being fruitful?
- What illustrations from the Old Testament shows fruitfulness?
- How does the Cross bring fruitfulness in our lives?

What does fruitfulness look like?

Let's look at several types of fruitfulness.

Physical fruitfulness of humanity in the world

> **From creation**: *"So God created man in His own image; in the image of God, He created him; male and female He created them. (28) Then God blessed them, and God said to them, "Be fruitful and multiply; fill the earth and subdue it; have dominion over the fish of the sea, over the birds of the air, and over every living thing that moves on the earth."* (*Genesis 1:27-28 NKJV*)

Noah: *"So God blessed Noah and his sons and said to them: "Be fruitful and multiply, and fill the earth." (Genesis 9:1 NKJV)*

After the world became repopulated, the Lord picked out a particular person to bless and promised he would become a father of many nations.

Abraham: *"No longer shall your name be called Abram, but your name shall be Abraham; for I have made you a father of many nations. (6) "I will make you exceedingly fruitful; and I will make nations of you, and kings shall come from you."* (*Genesis 17:5-6*)

Abraham had one son of the promise. There was only one – don't see much fruitfulness here.

Isaac: *"And the LORD appeared to him the same night and said, "I am the God of your father Abraham; do not fear, for I am with you. I will bless you and multiply your descendants for My servant Abraham's sake."* (*Genesis 26:24*)

Now we have two sons – this is going to take a long time.

Jacob/Israel: (Genesis 28:3-5) Isaac's blessing on Jacob – May God bless you and make you fruitful and multiply you. (Israel - Genesis 35:9-11) God changes Jacob to Israel. Be fruitful and multiply.

Okay, twelve is a more significant number – this is growing.

12 sons and their families enter Egypt which numbered 70. (Genesis 46:27)and they continued to grow. (Exodus 1:1-7) – They stayed in Egypt for 430 years.

By the time of the Exodus: Israel's men of war over 20 years old, counted to be 603,550. (Numbers 1:46) It is estimated that 25% of the population are in the military. Therefore: 4 x 603,550 = 2,414,200 people were leaving Egypt after that first Passover.

Wow! At the time of the Exodus, over 2 million people from that one man, Abraham.

The sand of the sea and stars in the sky: *"Therefore from one man (Abraham), and him as good as dead, were born as many as the stars of the sky in multitude--innumerable as the sand which is by the seashore."* (*Hebrews 11:12 NKJV*)

God blessed the nation of Israel with physical growth, but the Lord desires that there would be a physical fruitfulness in the church.

Physical fruitfulness of the Spirit, the visible church
Consider how the Christian church grew. It started with one, Jesus.

Jesus:
   12 disciples (Matthew 10:1)
   70 (Luke 10:1, 17)
   120 (Acts 1:15)
   500 (1 Corinthians 15:1-6)
   After the Holy Spirit is poured out upon Peter and the rest. Peter preaches the Gospel:
   3000 believed at Pentecost: (Acts 2:41-47) Peter's first sermon: **3,000** believed, then daily added to the church.
   Then a little later, Peter preached the Gospel again:

> **5,000** *believed. "Now as they (John and Peter) spoke to the people, the priests, the captain of the temple, and the Sadducees came upon them, (2) being greatly disturbed that they taught the people and preached in Jesus - the resurrection from the dead. (3) And they laid hands on them, and put them in custody until the next day, for it was already evening. (4) However, many of those who heard the Word believed; and the number of the men came to be about five thousand."* (*Acts 4:1-4 NKJV*)

It is not just about numbers: The Lord is concerned about one person as well:

> **Philip and the Ethiopian Eunuch** - *Act 8:26-40 - "Then Philip opened his mouth and, beginning at this Scripture (Isaiah 53): preached Jesus to him."* (*Acts 8:35 NKJV*)

It was through the Gospel message (Jesus' death, burial, and resurrection) that changed hearts, and the church grew.

Question 1: How does the church grow today? Do you believe that the message of the Gospel still changes hearts and is sufficient?

_____

_____

_____

_____

_____

Or does church growth come from smoke machines, flashing lights, and feel-good messages "I'm okay – you're okay. God loves everyone."

There is POWER in the Gospel that is to be preached from every passage in the Bible. Jesus, the Cross, and resurrection is our only hope.

I would suggest the study and book called "The Gospel for the Church," by Erick Hurt.

This study can be found at https://settingcaptivesfree.com/course/gospel-church or order the book at https://amzn.to/3xC5S6C

Spiritual fruitfulness of the Holy Spirit in the individual

> *"But the fruit of the Spirit is love, joy, peace, longsuffering, kindness, goodness, faithfulness, (23) gentleness, self-control. Against such there is no law."* (*Galatians 5:22-23 NKJV*)

> *"Either make the tree good, and its fruit good, or else make the tree bad and its fruit bad; for a tree is known by its fruit."* (*Matthew 12:33 NKJV*)

Question 2: What kind of fruit is evident in your life? What reputation of displaying the fruit of the Spirit, characteristics of Jesus, do you have?

_____

_____

_____

_____

_____

Consider Jesus' parable of the Seed and the Four Soils briefly

The Seed and the four soils

(Matthew 13:1-9; 18-23; Mark 4:1-9; 13-20 Luke 8:4-8; 11-15)

Seed: Word of God, Word of the kingdom (remember all Scriptures point us to Jesus. John 5:39) Like Philip did with the Ethiopian Eunuch

Soils: Different Heart conditions

Wayside path: devil steals the Word (blinds the eyes); that person does not understand it.

> *"whose minds the god of this age has blinded, who do not believe,*
> *lest the light of the gospel of the glory of Christ, who is the image*
> *of God, should shine on them." (2 Corinthians 4:4 NKJV)*

Rocky soil: the person believe with joy – but no roots – They will fall away after tribulation or persecution because of the Word.

> *"But everyone who hears these sayings of Mine, and does not do*
> *them, will be like a foolish man who built his house on the sand:*
> *(27) "and the rain descended, the floods came, and the winds*
> *blew and beat on that house; and it fell. And great was its fall."*
> *(Matthew 7:26-27 NKJV)*

Thorny soil: these people are choked with the cares, riches, and pleasures of life – they produce no fruit, they are unfruitful.

> *"for Demas has forsaken me, having loved this present world, and has departed for Thessalonica--."* (*2 Timothy 4:10 NKJV*)

> *"Not everyone who says to Me, 'Lord, Lord,' shall enter the kingdom of heaven, but he who does the will of My Father in heaven. (22) "Many will say to Me in that day, 'Lord, Lord, have we not prophesied in Your name, cast out demons in Your name, and done many wonders in Your name?' (23) "And then I will declare to them, 'I never knew you; depart from Me, you who practice lawlessness!'"* (*Matthew 7:21-23 NKJV*)

> *"Do not love the world or the things in the world. If anyone loves the world, the love of the Father is not in him. (16) For all that is in the world--the lust of the flesh, the lust of the eyes, and the pride of life--is not of the Father but is of the world."* (*1 John 2:15-16 NKJV*)

For further study:
(Luke 12:15, 21; Luke 18:24; 1 Timothy 6:9-10)

Good soil: these people heard and believed – they bear much fruit—some hundred, sixty, thirty.

> *"He came to His own, and His own did not receive Him. (12) But as many as received Him, to them He gave the right to become children of God, to those who believe in His name: (13) who were born, not of blood, nor of the will of the flesh, nor of the will of man, but of God."* (*John 1:11-13 NKJV*)

> *"being filled with the fruits of righteousness which are by Jesus Christ, to the glory and praise of God."* (*Philippians 1:11 NKJV*)

"that you may walk worthy of the Lord, fully pleasing Him, being fruitful in every good work and increasing in the knowledge of God." (*Colossians 1:10 NKJV*)

"But grow in the grace and knowledge of our Lord and Savior Jesus Christ. To Him be the glory both now and forever. Amen." (*2 Peter 3:18 NKJV*)

For further study:
(Romans 6:22; 7:4; Ephesians 5:9; Philippians 1:11; Colossians 1:10)
Each person is some type of soil. There are only four options.

Question 3: Which soil type would you consider yourself - Wayside path, rocky, thorny, or good? How would you categorize your fruitfulness? Why?

Illustration from the Old Testament:
Consider the promise made to the Messiah (Jesus) in the OT about being fruitful.

"Yet it pleased the LORD to bruise [crush] Him (Jesus); He (the Father) has put Him (Jesus) to grief. When You (the Father) make His (Jesus') soul an offering for sin, He (Jesus) shall see His (Jesus') seed, [Hebrews 12:1-2] He (the Father) shall prolong His (Jesus') days [resurrection], And the pleasure of the LORD (the Father) shall prosper in His (Jesus') hand. (11) He (the Father) shall see the labor of His (Jesus') soul, and be satisfied. By His (the Father's) knowledge, My righteous Servant (Jesus) shall justify many, For He (Jesus) shall bear their iniquities." (*Isaiah 53:10-11 NKJV*)

"A posterity [our children, a seed, their descendants, a whole generation, His spiritual seed] shall serve Him. It will be recounted of the Lord to the next generation, (31) They will come and declare His righteousness to a people who will be born, That He has done this." (Psalm 22:30-31 NKJV)

Jesus' fruitfulness ought to be seen here in His church. Both in character and numbers. Pray to be used by the Lord to grow His church. Pray that you would be fruitful.

Question 4: What are you doing in your church to help in the people's growth and reaching others with the Gospel?

_____

_____

_____

_____

_____

Application: How can you be fruitful?

"I am the true Vine, and My Father is the vinedresser. (2) "Every branch in Me that does not bear fruit He takes away; and every branch that bears fruit He prunes, that it may bear more fruit. (3) "You are already clean because of the Word which I have spoken to you. (4) "Abide in Me, and I in you. As the branch cannot bear fruit of itself, unless it abides in the Vine, neither can you, unless you abide in Me. (5) "I am the Vine, you are the branches. He who abides in Me, and I in him, bears much fruit; for without Me, you can do nothing. (6) "If anyone does not abide in Me, he is cast out as a branch and is withered; and they gather them and throw them into the fire, and they are burned. (7) "If you

abide in Me, and My words abide in you, you will ask what you
desire, and it shall be done for you. (8) "By this, My Father is
glorified, that you bear much fruit; so you will be My disciples."
(John 15:1-8 NKJV)

Consider with me this illustration:

WHERE DOES THE VINE STOP AND THE BRANCH START?
In John 15, Jesus reminds us by using this illustration of the Vine and the branches, that we are to abide in Him and that He abides in us. Because of the Cross, we have been crucified with Christ, and we find that we are now genuinely alive and fruitful. (Galatians 2:20)

Look at the picture: when asked to point out the Vine or the branch, that is pretty easy. But where does one stop and the other start?

The closer we look; it becomes tough to say when that transition takes place. There becomes a blur of distinction. All that we can say is that they are abiding together.

I think this is reflected in this passage:

"Now when they saw the boldness of Peter and John, and perceived that they were uneducated and untrained men, they marveled. And they realized that they had been with Jesus." (*Acts 4:13 NKJV*)

Like the branch that is abiding in the Vine, we also begin to reflect the Vine. We are becoming more and more conformed to that image of the Vine.

"But we all, with unveiled face, beholding as in a mirror the glory of the Lord, are being transformed into the same image from glory to glory, just as by the Spirit of the Lord." (2 Corinthians 3:18 NKJV)

We place ourselves at the foot of the Cross and behold Jesus hanging from the Cross. He is loving us, dying for us, taking upon Himself our sins, and bleeding out His life's blood to cover our sins. There at the Cross, we find our identity. By faith, we also find ourselves crucified with Him, and then we died with Him. But there in the tomb, as Jesus' dead body lies, on the third day, He rose victorious over sin, death, and the devil.

We, too, rose with Him as new creatures in Christ. As we abide in Him, we find that our lives are radically changed for His glory.

"If you abide in Me, and My words abide in you, you will ask what you desire, and it shall be done for you. (8) "By this My Father is glorified, that you bear much fruit; so you will be My disciples." (*John 15:7-8 NKJV*).

That time in God's Word and praying that Word back to the Father will bear much fruit and bring glory to the Father.

When people look, do they see that you have been with Jesus like Peter and John? Not that we have some great insight or knowledge of the Bible, but that we have been in the presence of God. We can see the results of "being in the vine"- *fruit*. That intimacy that we have with Jesus, the oneness that we have with Him, will be seen by others, and they will marvel and realize that we have been with Jesus.

Question 5: When people look, do they see that you have been with Jesus like Peter and John? What would your friends say about your Christianity?

If you are abiding in Christ – what are your words like?

Word – Jesus would say those same words I am saying in love, joy, peace, longsuffering, kindness, goodness, faithfulness, gentleness, self-control.

> *"The law of the LORD is perfect, converting the soul; The testimony of the LORD is sure, making wise the simple; (8) The statutes of the LORD are right, rejoicing the heart; The commandment of the LORD is pure, enlightening the eyes; (9) The fear of the LORD is clean, enduring forever; The judgments of the LORD are true and righteous altogether. (10) More to be desired are they than gold, Yea, than much fine gold; Sweeter also than honey and the honeycomb. (11) Moreover, by them, Your servant is warned, And in keeping them, there is great reward. (12) Who can understand his errors? Cleanse me from secret faults. (13) Keep back Your servant also from presumptuous sins; Let them not have dominion over me. Then I shall be blameless, And I shall be innocent of great transgression. (14) Let the words of my mouth and the meditation of my heart Be acceptable in Your sight, O LORD, my strength and my Redeemer." (Psalm 19:7-14 NKJV)*

> *"But no man can tame the tongue. It is an unruly evil, full of deadly poison. (9) With it we bless our God and Father, and with it we curse men, who have been made in the similitude of God.*

(10) Out of the same mouth proceed blessing and cursing. My brethren, these things ought not to be so. (11) Does a spring send forth fresh water and bitter from the same opening? (12) Can a fig tree, my brethren, bear olives, or a grapevine bear figs? Thus, no spring yields both saltwater and fresh." (James 3:8-12 NKJV)

Why are you letting gossip set the tone of your words? Why are you letting secular TV programs set the tone of your words? Why do you allow those websites catering to the flesh to set the tone of your words? Why do you need some profanity or curse words to accent your words?

Are your words filtered through the Cross? Are you standing before the Cross and speak words that reflect Jesus' words? Do your words show: love, joy, peace, longsuffering, kindness, goodness, faithfulness, gentleness, self-control?

Question 7: If you are abiding in Christ – what are your words like?

_____

_____

_____

_____

_____

If you are abiding in Christ – what are your actions or deeds like?

Deed – Jesus would do the very same thing I am doing in love, joy, peace, longsuffering, kindness, goodness, faithfulness, gentleness, self-control.

"But we all, with unveiled face, beholding as in a mirror the glory of the Lord, are being transformed into the same image from glory to glory, just as by the Spirit of the Lord." (2 Corinthians 3:18 NKJV)

Why are you letting gossip set the tone of your actions? Why are you letting secular TV programs set the tone of your activities? Why do you allow those websites catering to the flesh to set the tone of your actions?

Are your actions filtered through the Cross? Are you standing before the Cross and doing what reflects Jesus' actions? Do your actions show: love, joy, peace, longsuffering, kindness, goodness, faithfulness, gentleness, self-control?

Question 8: If you are abiding in Christ – what are your actions or deeds like?

Keys to Abiding in the Vine.

Are you in the Word daily?

Read and meditate on that Word? Do you see Jesus in that Scripture you're reading?

Do you stop, check off that box? Or continue to think about that Word and the application of the Cross as you wash in the blood, as you walk in the Spirit, as you war against your flesh?

Question 9: How would you describe your time in the Word?

Are you praying daily?

Praying after reading the Word. Praying that Word back to God.

Do you stop, check off that box? Or do you continue to pray throughout the day? Applying the Cross in your prayers as you wash in the blood, as you walk in the Spirit, as you war against your flesh?

Question 10: How would you describe your time in prayer?

_____

_____

_____

_____

_____

Come to the Cross and look up – Look at the Cross with me.

There nailed to the top of the Cross – Jesus' crime: "The King of the Jews." (Matthew 27:37; Mark 15:26; Luke 23:38; John 19:19)

If you are crucified with Jesus – what crimes would be listed?

Adultery, fornication, uncleanness, lewdness, idolatry, sorcery, hatred, contentions, jealousies, outbursts of wrath, selfish ambitions, dissensions, heresies, envy, murders, drunkenness, revelries, and the like;

Jesus took these upon Himself for you – your crimes became Jesus' crimes.

As the soldiers strip Jesus of His clothes – He is nailed to the Cross and lifted up: (Psalm 22:18; Matthew 27:35)

Look up:

- Look at the crown of thorns, blood running down His face (Matthew 27:29; Mark 15:17)
- Look at the face, distorted by beatings, beard pulled out, eyes swollen, beyond recognition. (Isaiah 50:6; Isaiah 52:14; Matthew 26:67)
- Look at His back torn apart by the whips, like furrows plowed in His back. See the bones through the torn flesh like hamburger. (Psalm 22:17; Psalm 129:3)

- Look at the nails in His hands – stretched out (Psalm 22:16)
- Look at the nail in His feet – holding up His weight. (Psalm 22:14)
- Look at Jesus lifting up His body to catch a breath as His back rubs against that rugged Cross.
- Look at your sins placed upon Jesus, that list of crimes that causes the Father to judge and pour out His wrath upon His Son. (Isaiah 53:4-6; 1 Peter 3:18)
- Look at the foot of the Cross – blood flowing down the Cross, blood pouring from His wounds. The blood of Jesus covers the ground. (Colossians 1:19-20)

Listen:

- Jesus prayed: *"Father, forgive them, for they do not know what they do"* (Luke 23:34)
- Jesus said: To His mother, "Woman, behold your son!" To John, "Behold your mother!" (John 19:26-27)
- Jesus said: to the believing thief, "Today, you will be with Me in Paradise." (Luke 23:43)
- Jesus cried out: My God, My God, why have You forsaken Me? (Psalm 22:1; Matthew 27:46; Mark 15:34)
- Jesus said: "I thirst!" "It is Finished!" (John 19:28-30)
- Jesus said: "Father into Your hands, I commit My spirit." And He died. (Luke 23:46)

The soldier thrust a spear into His side, into His heart; water and blood came out. (John 19:34)

Jesus was removed from the Cross. The nails were removed, and the body was wrapped and placed into a tomb. (Isaiah 53:9; Matthew 27:59-60; Mark 15:45-46; Luke:23:50-56; John 19:38-42)

Then on the third day – Jesus rose victorious over sin, death, and the devil. Yet, He still bore the marks of the Cross. (Matthew 28:1-8; Mark 16:1-8; Luke 24:1-12; John 20:1-10)

Can you stand there at the Cross and looking up at your Savior and continue in your sin? Let the Cross break your heart – continue looking and let the Cross heal your heart. The blood is sufficient to cover all of life. The blood will always wash. Come to the Cross, and there learn to walk in the Spirit.

Question 11: What effect has coming to the Cross had in your life through these lessons?

_____

_____

_____

_____

_____

Abide in Him… and walk in the Spirit that was given to you when you believed. Come to the Cross and find freedom from your sin.

Go, be fruitful, and multiply.

Testimony

*T*hank you for walking with me through these lessons. I'm looking forward to hearing from you today as you share your experience of the past 13 lessons.

I know I have shared my experience to some degree throughout this course. Still, I offer the following summary of the changes I have experienced by God's grace after learning to walk in the Spirit under the shadow of the Cross.

First, God has brought me into wonderful intimacy with Jesus, close union with Him walking by the Holy Spirit. Even when in tragedy, I was being comforted by the promises of the Gospel during these lessons. I had lost my youngest son to murder. Shawn was only 28 years old. I was completing lesson 11 when this happened. It was God's word and the promises that came with walking in the Spirit that continues to sustain me. I found that His grace is sufficient.

> *"And He said to me, "My grace is sufficient for you, for My strength is made perfect in weakness." Therefore most gladly I will rather boast in my infirmities, that the power of Christ may rest upon me." (2 Corinthians 12:9 NKJV)*

I have been reminding myself all through this course, "I have been crucified with Christ." I would remind myself in prayer as I laid in bed before going to sleep; I am crucified with Him. And before I got up as I awoke, again, I would pray to remind myself; I am crucified with Jesus.

> *"I have been crucified with Christ; it is no longer I who live, but Christ lives in me; and the life which I now live in the flesh I live by faith in the Son of God, who loved me and gave Himself for me." (Galatians 2:20 NKJV)*

Jesus loved me and gave Himself there on the Cross for me. My relationship with Jesus has grown as I went through these lessons myself.

Second, as I reflected on love, joy, peace, longsuffering, kindness, goodness, faithfulness, gentleness, and self-control, I saw that all of these qualities are given to me as I abide in Christ at the Cross. The Holy Spirit applied the cleansing blood to my life and gave me the power to live out these qualities. With that said, I am still growing and will not be complete until I see Jesus face to face. By His grace, I spend time daily in the Bible and pray.

> *"O God, You are my God; Early will I seek You; My soul thirsts for You; My flesh longs for You In a dry and thirsty land Where there is no water." (Psalm 63:1 NKJV)*

Third, I've been set free from the works of the flesh. The Cross has been set up to tear down those temptations as I flee to the Cross and am washed by the blood of the Lamb. I see that I am in a real battle, and the power of the Cross is greater than the flesh, sin, and the devil.

> *"And they overcame him by the blood of the Lamb and by the word of their testimony, and they did not love their lives to the death." (Revelation 12:11 NKJV)*

Fourth, this message of the Gospel (Jesus' death, burial, and resurrection) is not just for me. I am looking for opportunities to share the hope and joy I am finding because of what God has done in my life.

Fifth, I now have only one message to proclaim, "Jesus Christ and Him crucified. (1 Corinthians 2:2) I want to see others have the same excitement in sharing the only message that will set us free from the bondage of sin.

Look for ways to use these lessons to start a Bible study at your church or in your home. Look for ways that you can proclaim the power of the Gospel and see God work in the lives of others.

"I have proclaimed the good news of righteousness In the great assembly; Indeed, I do not restrain my lips, O LORD, You Yourself know. (10) I have not hidden Your righteousness within my heart; I have declared Your faithfulness and Your salvation; I have not concealed Your lovingkindness and Your truth From the great assembly." (Psalm 40:9-10 NKJV)

Now I'm eager to hear from you. What changes have you experienced?

Continue to the next section, where you'll have the opportunity to share your experience.

Congratulations on completing this course.

We've covered a lot of ground together walking through these lessons. I've been a learner/sharer just like you, like one beggar sharing bread with another. Thank you for allowing me to share the gospel of Jesus Christ with you.

It's been a true honor to walk with you, friend, to encourage you to keep your eyes on Jesus, to learn from the things you've shared, and to praise and worship God with you.

I hope you've had an opportunity to reflect on your journey through this course and are ready to share your thoughts.

Question 1: What did you find most encouraging as you went through these lessons?

Question 2: How has the principles of being crucified with Christ, and walking in the Spirit help fight against the works of the flesh?

_____

_____

_____

_____

_____

Today is your opportunity to share your journey through this course. Did you experience change?

Please take your time and share your experience of the past 13 lessons of walking through these lessons. Did you come to the cross in these lessons and see the fruit growing? Did you learn to walk by the Spirit and to war against your flesh? Did God give you a plan that you implemented? We are interested in hearing about any changes in your life since you started taking this course.

Question 3: What changes have taken place in your life over the previous 13 lessons?

_____

_____

_____

_____

_____

Thank you for sharing.

Additional studies can be found online at www.settingcaptivesfree.com.

www.ingramcontent.com/pod-product-compliance
Lightning Source LLC
LaVergne TN
LVHW061223060426
835509LV00012B/1396